J. R. R. TOLKIEN

MODERN LITERATURE SERIES

GENERAL EDITOR: Philip Winsor

In the same series:

J. R. R. TOLKIEN

Katharyn F. Crabbe

FREDERICK UNGAR PUBLISHING CO.
NEW YORK

To My Mother

Library of Congress Cataloging in Publication Data

Crabbe, Katharyn F., 1945–

    J.R.R. Tolkien.

    (Modern literature series)
    Bibliography: p.
    Includes index.
    1. Tolkien, J. R. R. (John Ronald Reuel), 1892–
1973.   2. Authors, English—20th century—Biography.
I. Series: Modern literature monographs.

PR6039.032Z623	828'.91209 [B]	81-4793
ISBN 0-8044-2134-X		AACR2
ISBN 0-8044-6091-4 (pbk.)		

Contents

Chronology

1892   Born in Bloemfontein, Orange Free State (now South Africa).

1895   Mother returns to England with Tolkien and brother.

1896   Father dies.

1904   Mother dies.

1911   Wins a scholarship to Oxford University to study classics.

1915   Takes a First Class degree in English from Oxford. Enters the army.

1916   Marries Edith Bratt. Serves at the Battle of the Somme. Is invalided out of the army in November.

1917   Begins to write *The Silmarillion*. First son, John, is born.

1918   Joins the staff of the *Oxford English Dictionary*.

1920   Appointed Reader in English Language at Leeds University. Second son, Michael, is born.

1924   Third son, Christopher, is born.

1925   Publishes an edition of *Sir Gawain and the Green Knight* with E. V. Gordon. Is named Rawlinson and Bosworth Professor of Anglo-Saxon at Oxford University.

1929   Daughter, Priscilla, is born.

1936   Lectures on *Beowulf:* "The Monsters and the Critics."

1937   Publishes *The Hobbit*.

Introduction

Defending the integrity of the literature he called "fairy-stories" against proponents of those varieties of literature that seek to represent "real life," J. R. R. Tolkien wrote, "Why should a man be scorned if, finding himself in prison, he tries to get out and go home? Or if, when he cannot do so, he thinks and talks about topics other than jailers and prison-walls?" Had he wished to write of "jailers and prison-walls," Tolkien could have found abundant material in his own life to provide plots and incidents for novels in the mold of *Oliver Twist,* or, in a more modern vein, for ironic little stories of men who lead lives of quiet desperation. Orphaned at an early age, dependent for his education on scholarships and the support of a benefactor, kept for several years from association with the woman he loved by the wishes of that same benefactor, and graduated from university just in time to participate in the Battle of the Somme, one of the bloodiest tragedies of World War I, Tolkien had opportunities early and often to observe and to experience the depressing, frustrating, and limiting possibilities of modern life as well as the joyous, fulfilling, and liberating. But Tolkien's imaginative faculty was not inclined toward the careful recreation of the world around him or the slow building up of detail that creates recognizably real characters or settings. Rather, his was a mythopoetic imagination, one that created a mythology as it worked, and Middle-earth, the subject matter and inspiration of the mythology he created, became the home to which the prisoner longed to return.

As is true of mythologies of much greater antiq-uity, Tolkien's tales of Middle-earth take place years and miles away from the modern reader; but as is true also of other mythologies, the tales are psy-chologically as close to us as we can wish or as we can bear. His tales of elves, dwarves, hobbits, and men are not about our world in the sense that they are about Europe or Africa, or shortages of natural resources, or the threat of nuclear disaster; they are about us in the sense that they are about good and evil, sorrow, pain, injustice, and sometimes heroism, and even joy. They are, that is, not so much about what is real as they are about what is true. The difference between the two is a difference that Tolkien's life, from his earliest years, taught him to appreciate.

1

~~~~~~

The Quest as Life

John Ronald Reuel Tolkien was the first son and the first child of Arthur Reuel Tolkien and Mabel Suffield Tolkien. Arthur Tolkien was a banker by profession, first with Lloyds Bank, and then, when promotions and advancement came too slowly at Lloyds for a man who wanted to marry and raise a family, with the Bank of Africa in Bloemfontein, capital of the Orange Free State, a part of what is now South Africa. His family were German by descent and had been piano manufacturers in Birmingham until Arthur Tolkien's father's bankruptcy. Thus, though the family had been solid members of the middle class in earlier years, by the time of J. R. R. Tolkien's birth, the Tolkiens were in reduced circumstances.

Mabel Suffield Tolkien was the daughter of John Suffield, once an independent draper in Birmingham and proud of his heritage as a native of the Midlands, the central region of England. As a lover of all that was English, he was no doubt something less than delighted when his daughter proposed to sail to Africa to marry the son of a bankrupt, but nonetheless, the two were married on April 16, 1891 in Cape Town. J. R. R. Tolkien was born on January 3, 1892 and his brother, Hilary Arthur Reuel Tolkien, was born on February 17, 1894.

Although Arthur Tolkien enjoyed life in the Orange Free State and prospered in his position at the Bank of Africa, Mabel disliked almost everything about Bloemfontein: the weather (too hot in the summer, too dry and windy in the winter), the society (boring and limited to bank acquaintances), and the landscape (too barren). But she persevered until it became clear that the intense heat of the summers was undermining the health of her eldest son. Then, in April of 1895, she and the children returned to Birmingham, Arthur planning to join them later.

The return to the more moderate climes of England did serve to improve the health of the child, but as he became stronger, his father became weaker. In November of 1895, not a year after his family's departure, Arthur Tolkien was stricken with rheumatic fever, a disease usually suffered by children and accompanied by a high fever, swelling of the joints, and inflammation of the heart. When her husband had not recovered by January, Mabel decided that she and her sons must return to Africa to care for him. However, before they could embark, news came that Arthur had suffered a severe hemorrhage, and by February 15, 1896, he was dead.

After recovering from the shock and the guilt that accompanied her husband's death, Mabel began to organize the life of her family with admirable competence. Her requirements and those of her sons were few, but so were their resources: They must have a cheap, but not a squalid, place to live, and the boys must have access to a good education. The cheap though not squalid lodging was a semidetached row house in Sarehole, a small village just outside Birmingham. J. R. R. Tolkien loved Sarehole—it had everything a small energetic boy could want: fields, trees, a river and a mill, countryside to explore, and dells in which to picnic. So the lodging question was settled.

As for education, Mabel, who had a well-developed talent for Latin, French, and German, as well as for drawing and painting, undertook to bring her sons to a level of achievement that would allow them to pass the entrance examinations for the King Edward VI School in Birmingham, an excellent grammar school and, nearly as important, Arthur Tolkien's old school. Tolkien fell in love with languages from the moment he met them. He took immediately to Latin when his mother introduced it, though many years later he wrote, "Latin—to express new sensations that are still vivid in memory . . . —seemed so *normal* that pleasure or distaste was equally inapplicable." He also began to learn French at this early age, but he liked it less than Latin or English because he found in it fewer "words in which there is pleasure in the contemplation of form and sense."[1]

Under his mother's tutelage Tolkien also began to develop the idiosyncratic style of handwriting that stayed with him throughout his life and to cultivate his talent in drawing. Both the elaborate and precise lettering and the taste and talent for drawing and painting, especially landscapes, contributed to *The Hobbit* and *The Lord of the Rings* when Tolkien began to illustrate his fictions.

All was not work, however, and although Tolkien was sometimes a lazy student, he was always an avid reader, especially of the tales and myths of American Indians and of fairy tales. Humphrey Carpenter records that Tolkien's favorite story as a child was the Norse myth of Sigurd the Völsung and the death of the dragon Fafnir who guarded the treasure of the Völsungs. Tolkien was so excited by the idea of dragons and the wonder of the nameless north that at age seven he began to write his own story about dragons. Years later, recalling the charm and wonder of Fafnir, he said, "I desired dragons with a profound desire."[2]

For the first few years after his father's death, life was kind to Tolkien and to his brother. But in 1900 two important changes intruded into the idyllic life where study and pleasure, home and society, discipline and freedom were intertwined. First, in June of that year, Mabel Tolkien converted to Catholicism and began to instruct her sons in its beliefs and practices. Second, Tolkien passed the entrance examination and entered the King Edward VI School. As if that was not upset enough, these changes engendered more changes. Both the Suffield family, who were Methodists and Anglicans, and the Tolkiens, who were Baptists, strongly objected to Catholicism. Mabel paid for her religious decision in cash, as financial help from the Suffield side declined, but she would not recant. Thus, her two sons became increasingly cut off from their roots.

The effects of entering school were equally disruptive. For Tolkien to attend the King Edward School was important for two reasons: It was his father's school, and it was the best school in Birmingham. Mabel Tolkien knew that her son was bright, and she knew that he was inclined to be lazy. More important, she knew that his only hope for a university education lay in winning a scholarship. Therefore, he had to have the best grammar school education available. Tolkien was willing enough to try, but the school was located in the center of Birmingham, about four miles away from the village of Sarehole. Trams did not run all the way to Sarehole, and even if they had, he could not have afforded the daily fare. So near the end of the year 1900, the three Tolkiens left Sarehole for a house in Birmingham, nearer the school and nearer a Catholic church. Tolkien never returned to idyllic country life, but the memory of Sarehole is evoked in the rural scenes of nearly all his works.

At the King Edward School, then at St. Philip's School (affiliated with the Catholic church), Tolkien began to discover the extent of his academic talent. By 1902 it was clear that only the King Edward School could challenge him, so he returned to classes there in the fall of 1903 as a scholarship boy. At King Edward he discovered Greek ("the fluidity of Greek, punctuated by hardness, and with its surface glitter captivated me, even when I met it first only in Greek names, of history and mythology, and I tried to invent a language that would embody the Greekness of Greek")[3] and Middle English in the form of the *Canterbury Tales* to complement the Latin, French, and German his mother had taught him, and the Welsh he had found dancing along on the railroad cars that rumbled past his home.

In the fall of 1904, when Tolkien was twelve, his mother, who had suffered for several years with diabetes, died. Her death was a great blow to her sons. It seems clear that Tolkien associated his mother with the Catholic church, as nine years after her death he wrote: "My own dear mother was a martyr indeed, and it is not to everybody that God grants so easy a way to his great gifts as he did to Hilary and myself, giving us a mother who killed herself with labour and trouble to ensure us keeping the faith."[4]

At her death, Mabel Tolkien left her sons eight hundred pounds invested in securities, the memory of idyllic days in rural England, and the guardianship of Father Francis Morgan, their parish priest and faithful friend. In this last the boys were lucky, for rather than having to return to what might well have

been the disapproval and religious recriminations of
the Suffield or Tolkien family households, they were
able to maintain some small continuities—their
schools, their church, their friends. Father Morgan
supplemented their income and kept them in the
King Edward School, and he found lodgings for
them near the Oratory, which allowed them to spend
some time with him.

In addition to providing the means for Tolkien
to continue his studies, Father Morgan was, in a
way, responsible for the other major influence in
Tolkien's life: his marriage. When Father Morgan
arranged for the two boys to lodge near him, he
settled them in the home of a Mrs. Faulkner, where
another orphan, Edith Bratt, was already a resident.
Miss Bratt was small and dark, with grey eyes and a
talent for music that, had she not married, might
have led her to a career as a music teacher or, possibly, as a concert pianist.[5] When she and Tolkien met,
she was nineteen years old, he sixteen.

Now, seventy-five years later, an attraction between two orphans living in the same house seems, if
not inevitable, at least understandable. But for
Father Morgan, who must have understood that
Tolkien's only path to advancement led through a
long and demanding education, it was unthinkable.
Therefore, contact between the two was forbidden,
and Edith was sent away from Mrs. Faulkner's.[6]

Though there is some evidence that the two
young people felt the forced separation deeply, there
is none suggesting that they attempted to defy their
guardians or to subvert their intentions deliberately.
But if they were not defiant, neither were they ac-
quiescent: Having vowed to be true to one another,
they waited, patiently or impatiently, but at least
quietly, until Edith reached twenty-one, the age of
majority. Meanwhile, Tolkien finished his under-

graduate education and earned his First Class degree in English Languages and Literature.

From the early days at the King Edward School, study clearly promised to become the center of Tolkien's life. With the guidance of his schoolmasters, he began to study linguistics and expanded his reading knowledge to include Anglo-Saxon (the language of the Germanic people in England before 1100), more Middle-English dialects (especially West Midlands, which was the dialect of his Suffield ancestors), and Old Norse (the original language of the story of Sigurd and Fafnir). He also learned some Spanish (to please Father Morgan) and some Gothic (an archaic language of the Germanic people who conquered most of the Roman Empire in the third, fourth, and fifth centuries), and he used these languages to extend and enrich his own invented languages. When in 1910 he took up debating at school, he found the custom of holding debates in Latin much too dull for his taste, and at various times debated in Greek, in Gothic, and in Anglo-Saxon, all of which amused his friends very much, though one may suspect that his opponents may not have appreciated the humor of it.[7]

However, it was not just the access to more and more languages that made the school society important to Tolkien. The all-male society of the King Edward School provided the first (and perhaps the most important) of the likeable, clubby, clever fellowships that were important in Tolkien's life and in his fictions. With a group of like-minded friends, Christopher Wiseman, R. Q. Gilson, and later Geoffrey B. Smith, he formed the Tea Club and Barrovian Society. In this unofficial club, members amused one another and themselves by sharing their intellectual and creative enthusiasms. Tolkien, for example, entertained his friends with recitations from the Old

and Middle-English poems he had discovered on his
own: *Beowulf, Pearl,* and *Sir Gawain and the Green
Knight.*

Throughout his life Tolkien repeatedly or-
ganized or was drawn into clubs—groups of men
whose interests and talents were similar to his own. As
an Oxford undergraduate, he started the Apolaus-
ticks, a group of freshmen who gave papers, held
discussions and debates, and ate good dinners. As a
Reader in English Language at Leeds University, he
joined with E. V. Gordon, another faculty member, in
instituting the Viking Club for undergraduates with
whom they met to drink beer, read the Old Norse
heroic tales called sagas, and sing drinking songs. In
the early days at Oxford, it was the Coalbiters, a
group who came together to read Icelandic sagas.
And finally it was the now famous Inklings, the group
that gathered around C. S. Lewis and Charles Williams to read and criticize one another's unpublished
works.

In the friendly, supportive, beer- and tobacco-
filled atmosphere of these gatherings, Tolkien
absorbed the outlines of social organizations that
comprise his sense of good in his fantasies. Indeed, in
the fellowship of the ring itself and in the elvish
Rivendell, the comfort of the hearth is more akin to
that of an English pub than that of a private home.

However, of all the tea clubs, drinking societies,
and literary groups to which Tolkien ever belonged,
the most important, in terms of the effect on his
literary imagination, was the Tea Club and Barrovian
Society of his grammar school days, and much of the
reason for its preeminence lay in the membership.
Wiseman, Gilson, and Smith were part and parcel of
the happy success Tolkien enjoyed at school, and
they were part of his sense of himself as a special
person—an intelligent, interesting (and interested)

young man. Because his three friends were so much a part of his emerging identity, and because Gilson's and Smith's deaths were so violent and so early, the dissolution of the Tea Club and Barrovian Society in the trenches of World War I gave that society emotional and psychological resonances far stronger than those occasioned by the natural drifting away of one friend or another to new interests or another job.

Thanks, then, to his mother, his schoolmasters, and his three best friends, by the time Tolkien entered Oxford in 1911 he had a taste for the sensory attractions of language—the sounds and shapes of words; a taste for philology, the study of the structure and development of language; and a taste for the myths that belong to those languages he had studied.

Tolkien was able to enter Oxford University because he won, on his second attempt, a scholarship officially titled an Open Classical Exhibition to Exeter College. Although the award alone would not have provided enough for his university education, a school-leaving grant from the King Edward School and a little more help from Father Morgan made an Oxford education a real possibility. Now all he had to do was to earn a decent degree.

In his first year as an Oxford undergraduate, Tolkien was not as successful as he should have been. As a winner of an Open Classical Exhibition, he was to study classics, but he was no longer really interested in classical literature, so he did not apply himself to it with very much dedication. Instead, he spent most of his time and energy with Joseph Wright, the Professor of Comparative Philology who had written a primer of the Gothic language Tolkien bought while at King Edwards. Lack of self-discipline also kept him from attending church and confession regularly, and this in turn made him feel guilty and depressed. However, these negatives were more than offset by his discovery of Finnish. Being a long-time seeker of heroic tales from the middle ages, Tolkien already knew the stories of the *Kalevala,* the Finnish heroic epic with its tales of Vainamoinen, the bringer of blessings to men, and the creation of the Sampo, or axis of the world. But as much as he loved the stories, he had no idea what they sounded like in the original. When he had mastered enough Finnish to begin picking his way through the original, the effect was exhilarating: "It was like discovering a wine-cellar filled with bottles of amazing wine of a kind and flavour never tasted before."[8] Later, he invented a new language based on Finnish, which eventually appeared in *The Lord of the Rings* as High-Elven.

By the end of his first four terms at Oxford, when the first round of exams that would eventually lead to the coveted degree had to be taken, Tolkien was obviously a young man in the wrong place. Six weeks of pure hard work was sufficient to earn a Second Class ranking in the exams, but he needed and was expected to earn a First. Still, he did very well in his special subject, Comparative Linguistics. Thus, he and the head of Exeter College agreed, he might well think about becoming a philologist. And as the languages that interested him most at the time were Old and Middle English, and other Germanic languages, they also agreed that he should change from classics to English.

Changing from classics to English meant focusing on philology and Old and Middle English. Tolkien chose Old Norse as his special subject, a language he had already begun to learn on his own. Old Norse is the language of the Norwegians who left their homeland in the ninth century and sailed to Iceland (so it is sometimes called Old Icelandic). The great stories of Old Norse are the sagas and the two Eddas, the Prose or Younger Edda and the Poetic or

Elder Edda. The Elder Edda is a series of poems, some heroic (that is, concerned with the works of men) and some mythological (concerned with the works of gods). In the language and the stories of Old Norse, Tolkien found a great deal of pleasure and excitement.

To be young and brilliant and studying languages and books he loved may have seemed like paradise to Tolkien, but such paradises were shattered for all young Britons by the outbreak of war. Tolkien was still an Oxford undergraduate when war was declared against Germany in 1914. He did not immediately rush out to enlist as many of his age did because he wanted to finish his degree first. He had a good chance at the First-Class degree that would just about guarantee an academic position after the war, and he was torn between a desire for a secure future and a desire for the fellowship of those who had enlisted before him. As a compromise, he joined a training program that would allow him to prepare for the war immediately but postpone his enlistment until he had completed his degree.

Successfully gaining a First-Class degree in June of 1915, Tolkien quickly joined his regiment, the Lancashire Fusiliers, in which Geoffrey Smith also served, although in a different battalion. He and Edith had at first intended not to marry until he was "settled," but the terrifying probability of Tolkien's death in the war convinced them not to wait. They married on March 22, 1916, and on June 4, 1916, Tolkien left for France, just in time to be a part of "The Big Push" and the Battle of the Somme.

One knows from various sources something of the absolute horror of the Battle of the Somme: the long, feckless bombardment of German placements; the mud; the stench; the surrealistic destruction of the landscape; and most of all, the miscalculations of

British generals that caused the flower of British manhood to climb up out of the trenches and trudge directly into the fire of German machine guns. At the end of the first day, 20,000 Allied troups, R. Q. Gilson among them, had died in the first assault on the Somme.

Christopher Wiseman had joined the Navy, so he was not at the Battle of the Somme; but Tolkien and Goeffrey Smith were, and for them and others like them, the horror increased daily. The rain and the shelling and the feet of thousands of men turned the land into a sea of mud. Most traces of vegetation disappeared, and the trees that managed to remain standing looked like survivors of a forest fire—all leaves and bark stripped off or blown away. And there were corpses everywhere, bloated, stinking, disfigured or mutilated, with parts completely blown away.

After the first push of July 1, life on the Somme was an endless round of night marches, daybreak attacks, and costly withdrawals. It was enervating, exhausting, harrowing, and seemingly endless. And when the war ended for Tolkien, the end was only half a reward. First, he came down with "trench fever," a malady transmitted by lice and characterized by a rash, high fever, headache, and mental confusion. Trench fever is rarely fatal, but it is incapacitating, so Tolkien was shipped home to a hospital in Birmingham on November 8, 1916. While he was recuperating, the news came that Geoffrey Smith had died when the injuries he received from a bursting shell turned gangrenous.

Geoffrey Smith was the poet of the Tea Club and Barrovian Society. It was he who knew and loved the modern English poets with the same fervor and delight that Tolkien felt for his Anglo-Saxon and Middle-English poems such as *Beowulf* and *Sir*

Gawain and the Green Knight. And it was Smith who encouraged Tolkien in his own poetic attempts and who encouraged him to read William Morris and Algernon Swinburne whose poetic recreations of ages long past evoked medievalism in a way that presaged Tolkien's creations. The deaths of Smith and Gilson and the dissolution of the Tea Club and Barrovian Society were heavy blows to Tolkien, who is often quoted to the effect that "by the time I was 21, all but one of my best friends were dead."

In the latter half of the twentieth century, World War I has come to symbolize the line of demarkation between the old ways and the modern, between the innocent and the ironic, between youthful hope and vigor and exhausted acceptance. It did not mark for Tolkien any sudden education out of youthful optimism, for he had learned at his mother's death that the world can be tragic. Yet, as his mother remained with him at least partly because she was intimately connected with the Catholicism to which he was faithful, the Tea Club and Barrovian Society remained with him in the ideal of the male fellowship to which he also remained faithful.

Tolkien, then, had from youth a facility for languages that was observed and, perhaps more important, admired by the people who were emotionally most important to him in his early years—his mother and the members of the Tea Club and Barrovian Society. When a schoolmaster lent him an Anglo-Saxon dictionary or a friend sold him a Gothic grammar, we may feel that fortuitous circumstance, and maybe even coincidence, was intruding, but by that time Tolkien's interest in and facility for languages was clearly something more than a precocious child's attempts to gain approval. Tolkien himself has said, "An enormously greater number of children have what you might call a creative element in them than is usually supposed, and it isn't necessarily limited to certain things; they may not want to paint or draw, or have much music, but they nevertheless want to create something. And if the main mass of education takes a linguistic form, their creation will take a linguistic form."[9] That is, for Tolkien, languages and their study provided an outlet for his creativity and an affirmation of life, for an element of futurity is implicit in every creative act as well as a tie to the past.

When the war ended and life assumed as much normalcy as it was likely to do, the young couple were parents of a son, John, and Tolkien secured his first civilian job. In 1919, he gratefully accepted a position as a junior editor on the *Oxford English Dictionary* project. The *OED,* as it is called, is a historical dictionary, and the aim of its compilers was "to present in alphabetical series the words that have formed the English vocabulary from the time of the earliest records down to the present day, with all the relevant facts concerning their form, sense-history, pronunciation, and etymology."[10] To be selected even for a junior position on this project was an honor and an indication that Tolkien's abilities were appreciated by the Oxford intellectual community, but the position was clearly only temporary. It was a good first step to an academic career, but still only a first step. In addition, when Michael Tolkien was born in 1920, the young philologist had four mouths to feed.

An opportunity to return to the classroom, this time as a teacher, was not long in coming, however. In 1921, Tolkien accepted a position as Reader of English Language at the University of Leeds. In a department that was biased in favor of literature, Tolkien was hired to teach philology and Anglo-Saxon literature. Drive, intelligence, and the ability to engender interest in language study soon led to a

Tolkien-designed revision of the curriculum in English Language and Literature. While at Leeds he also published the first two scholarly works that established his reputation as a philologist and Anglo-Saxon scholar. The first, *A Middle English Vocabulary,* essentially a glossary for his old tutor, Kenneth Sisam's *Fourteenth Century Verse and Prose,* resulted in his promotion to Professor of English Language at Leeds—the youngest person to hold a professorship there. His second publication was an edition of the Middle-English poem, *Sir Gawain and the Green Knight,* for which he prepared the text, while his collaborator, E. V. Gordon, prepared the notes. This edition of the famous poem is still the standard edition used by graduate students and scholars in English throughout the world.

In 1925, on the basis of his excellent work with students and his superb scholarship, Tolkien was named Bosworth and Rawlinson Professor of Anglo-Saxon at Oxford. To be named to a professorship at any British university is a great honor, for there is usually only a single professor in each subject, the remaining staff being lecturers or readers, but to be named a professor at Oxford is honor compounded. So after only four years away, Tolkien returned to Oxford where he completed, over a long life, his best known works of fantasy and of scholarship—*The Hobbit, The Lord of the Rings,* an essay titled *Beowulf: The Monsters and the Critics,* and a lecture on fairy tales.

The return to Oxford was a great boon to Tolkien, but it was much less a joy to his wife. Edith liked Leeds; she enjoyed the relaxed society that they found among the younger academic families there, whereas in Oxford, friendliness and sociability seemed to have been snuffed out under the weight of tradition and a sense of the importance of the place itself. Nonetheless, the Tolkiens and their three sons, John, Michael, and Christopher, born in 1924, were soon ensconced in a house on Northmore Road in the city of Oxford.

Like many orphans, Tolkien was a loving and dedicated family man. He enjoyed taking his children for walks through his beloved Midlands countryside; he willingly helped with homework; he supervised religious training; and perhaps most important, he entertained by making up stories.

His friend and student, S. T. R. O. d'Ardenne, wrote of Tolkien at this period, "All his letters . . . tell of his concern about his children's health, their comfort, their future; how best he could help them to succeed in life, and how to make their lives as perfect as possible. He started by giving them a most pleasant childhood, creating for them the deep sense of home which had been denied to him. . . ."[11] At the same time, Tolkien worked long hours at his profession, for many British academics of the time, Tolkien among them, lived in a kind of genteel poverty that required one to accept all kinds of offers of extra work, such as reading examinations for other institutions, to help support a family. In the midst of such after-hours activity is said to have occurred that happy concatenation of events that led to Tolkien's first published fantasy: A sentence, "In a hole in the ground there lived a hobbit," popped into his head, and a blank page in an examination book appeared for him to write it on.

In 1926, when Tolkien had been back at Oxford for a year, another medievalist joined the English faculty. C. S. Lewis, who later became well-known for his literary studies (*The Allegory of Love*), his Christian apologetics (*The Problem of Pain*), his science fiction trilogy, and his Narnia series for children, almost immediately became an important source of friendship, stability, and intellectual and creative stimulus for Tolkien. In his book *The Four Loves*, Lewis discusses ideal friendship partly in terms of his relationship with Tolkien. What is important to friendship, Lewis asserts, is not that friends should agree on everything, but that they are delighted to find that they agree on some important things. He writes: "The man who agrees with us that some question, little regarded by others, is of great importance, can be our Friend. He need not agree with us about the answer."[12] This is perhaps as close as we need to come in the present study to the question of whether Lewis influenced Tolkien. The two men agreed that Christianity was important; though one was Anglican and the other was Catholic; they agreed that myth was important, though one called it *myth* and the other called it *faery;* and they agreed that literary study was important, though one was *lit* and the other was *lang*. Beyond that, it is perhaps best to let the two speak for themselves. In 1959 Lewis wrote to an American scholar who had proposed to study his influence on Tolkien, saying, "No one ever influenced Tolkien —you might as well try to influence a bandersnatch. We listened to his work, but could affect it only by encouragement. He has only two reactions to criticism; either he begins the whole work over again from the beginning or else takes no notice at all."[13] And Tolkien agreed: "The unpayable debt that I owe to him was not 'influence' as it is ordinarily understood, but sheer encouragement. He was for long my only audience. Only from him did I ever get the idea that my 'stuff' could be more than a private hobby."[14]

In addition to his individual importance to Tolkien as a friend and kindred spirit, Lewis was the center around which the "Inklings," an informal literary group whose members also included Charles Williams and Hugo Dyson, formed. It was to this group, during the thirties and forties, that Tolkien read chapters of his works in progress—first *The Hobbit,* and later *The Lord of the Rings.*

The Hobbit, which had its written origin on the blank page of the famous examination book, probably had its real genesis earlier, about the time the Tolkiens returned to Oxford. Tolkien's older sons remember hearing the story told rather than read in the study of their first Oxford house at 22 Northmore Road.[15] But whether the story was first told in the study of that house or read after tea in the evenings in the second Oxford house at 20 Northmore, as the youngest son, Christopher, claims, it might never have been completed and published had a happy coincidence not occurred.

Tolkien had stopped working on *The Hobbit* at the point where Bilbo entered the dragon's lair. By the time he reached that point, Tolkien's children had begun to outgrow the story, or at least they no longer wanted a story time in the evenings. So the manuscript was put aside until, in 1936, Elaine Griffiths, one of Tolkien's students and a family friend, mentioned to a publisher's representative from Allen and Unwin that Professor Tolkien had written a children's story that might be of interest to the house. Both the publisher's representative, Susan Dagnall, and the publisher's ten-year-old son, Rayner, loved the book, which was quickly finished and published on September 21, 1937.

The Hobbit sold well from the first, collecting adulatory reviews in both England and America, and selling out the first edition by Christmas. The money was no doubt welcome, and the adulation must have been rewarding, though Tolkien was a bit worried about the effect of a children's book on his reputation at Oxford.

Seeing the success with which *The Hobbit* met, Allen and Unwin immediately proposed that Tolkien publish another story about hobbits in order to catch the market at its height, so they wrote to ask if he had, by chance, any such story already completed. He didn't; what he did have was a great mass of manuscripts setting forth a mythology of the elves; an unfinished time-travel story he wrote for the Inklings, called "The Lost Road"; and a short story with a mock-heroic theme called "Farmer Giles of Ham." Each was fine in its own way, but what was wanted was more hobbits, so Tolkien agreed to try to write the sequel his publisher wanted.

At about this time, Tolkien was invited to give the Andrew Lang Lecture at the University of St. Andrews in March of 1939. Andrew Lang, who is perhaps best remembered for his collections of fairy tales for children, named for various colors (i.e., *The Blue Book*), was also an important force in the study of folklore that had burgeoned in the nineteenth century. At the time he was invited to give the Lang lecture, Tolkien had already begun to think about a lecture on the fairy-story, and he determined to finish that lecture for delivery at St. Andrews. In the course of preparing it, he came to doubt seriously the responsibility of what he had done in *The Hobbit*, especially in adopting a narrative voice that seemed to "talk down" to children in remarks such as this observation on Elrond, the Elf-King of Rivendell: "He comes into many tales, but his part in the story of Bilbo's great adventures is only a small one, though important, as you will see, if we ever get to the end of it." The Lang lecture, later published as "On Fairy-Stories," with its firm pronouncements on the seriousness of fairy-stories and their status as the home of fantasy, recovery, escape, and consolation, traces the line of demarcation between the coy narrative attitude in *The Hobbit* and the far more somber, heroic, and elevated style of the sequel that began as the adventures of Bilbo's son, Bingo, and ended as the heroic trilogy, *The Lord of the Rings.*

The new book was begun in December 1937[16], but its way to completion was as long and as tortuous as Frodo's way to the crack of Doom. Life remained hectic for the Tolkiens: Academic work continued to take first place in Tolkien's own life, as the demands for tutoring sessions, lectures, and faculty business showed no signs of decreasing. Their youngest son, Christopher, was sent home from boarding school, having been diagnosed, apparently incorrectly, as suffering from heart disease and requiring complete bed rest. And the threat of the coming war, and later the fact of that war, did nothing to smooth the path to publication for *The Lord of the Rings.* The greatest problem, however, was that the book kept growing. And with every additional chapter, the tone grew darker and more somber until at last Tolkien was not sure whether the book would ever be suitable for children at all.

Each time Tolkien was stymied by the plot, a new dark force would appear in the work to keep the game in play: The Black Riders, the Ring Wraiths, and Shelob. He wrote chapters and read them to C. S. Lewis and the Inklings. Then he stopped writing and planned and taught short courses to young men who came to Oxford before taking up duties as military officers. Christopher Tolkien, by now fully recovered from his schoolboy illness, was drafted and sent to South Africa, and his father wrote new chapters and sent him copies of them. Then committee or English faculty business required attention and he wrote nothing at all for some time. He revised, he rewrote; he revised *The Hobbit* to make the account of

Gollum and the Ring in the first work consistent with that of the new work. And twelve years later, in 1949, when the manuscript was finally complete, he precipitated a foolish quarrel with Stanley Unwin, forced Unwin to reject *The Lord of the Rings* by insisting that to take it he must also take the shapeless mass of narratives that was *The Silmarillion,* and changed publishers. It was late 1952 before he and the Unwin house resumed friendly relations, and it was 1954 before the first volume of *The Lord of the Rings* saw the light. But as with so many late fruits, it was the sweeter for the delay.

In the decade and a half the work had been in progress, it had grown so huge that it clearly could not be printed in a single volume. Yet, to print a nineteenth-century three-decker novel in 1954 seemed to be madness, because the costs of printing and paper were so high. On the other hand, Rayner Unwin, who as a ten-year-old had enthusiastically endorsed *The Hobbit,* pursuaded his father that though the work was "weird," it was a work that deserved publication. On the third hand, Unwin's earlier experience with Tolkien had taught them that he was likely to refuse any suggestions of extensive cuts. So Allen and Unwin made Tolkien an unusual offer: They would publish the work as three volumes, but instead of standard royalties, Tolkien would receive half of the profits. That is, he would receive nothing until expenses were met, but after the book had paid for itself, he and the publisher would share in the profits equally.

This arrangement proved to be a wonderful bit of luck for Tolkien, for *The Lord of the Rings* was a great success, and he drew far more from the profit sharing than he could have hoped to do from a percentage royalty. By early 1956 when he received his first royalty check from Allen and Unwin, his share of

the profits already amounted to more than 3,500
pounds, or roughly $14,000.[17] Sales continued to be
respectable throughout the fifties and early sixties,
and translations into Dutch, Swedish, and Polish appeared before the 1965 "War over Middle-earth"
signaled Tolkien's arrival as a cult hero.

In 1965 Ace Books, a paperback house specializ-
ing in science fiction, decided to take advantage of
the failure of U. S. copyright laws to protect foreign
authors by issuing an unauthorized edition of *The
Lord of the Rings*. Legally, if not morally, they could do
so without paying either Tolkien or Allen and Unwin
a single penny. The result was a flood of cheap editions placed in bookstores that catered to adoles-
cents and young adults, particularly college students.
The book that was neither a child's fantasy nor an
adult novel found its audience on the campuses of the
United States.

When an authorized edition was published by
Ballantine Books in 1965, members of Tolkien fan
clubs and the Science Fiction Writers of America re-
sponded to Tolkien's plea for ". . . courtesy (at least)
to living authors . . ."[18] and applied sufficient pres-
sure to Ace Books to cause them to offer to pay
royalties for every copy of the unauthorized version
that had been sold and to promise not to reprint once
stocks were depleted. By this time, the ready availabil-
ity of the cheap editions had combined with the
temper of the times to make the Tolkiens' future
secure. At least it assured them that following his
retirement from his professorship at Oxford, Tolkien would not have to worry about penury.

But the success of *The Lord of the Rings* was a
two-edged sword. It make Tolkien financially free,
but free to do what? The work that was on his mind,
that had been on his mind since his convalescence at
the end of World War I, the work about which he felt
so strongly that he could hardly bear to risk an

editor's rejection of it, was *The Silmarillion.* Certainly a financially secure retirement was the perfect opportunity to complete the long-cherished project. But, after all those years, the task of revising *The Silmarillion* into a unified whole must have been daunting. Where does one begin with a manuscript that has been growing by accretion for over forty years? How does one choose between early and late accounts of the same event or between prose and poetic versions? Assuming that one could complete these tasks, how would he bring forty years' worth of thinking about and discovering and modifying and seeing new sides of motivations and characters into a single vision? And finally, how would one approach the problem of bringing such a varied work into stylistic wholeness?

If the literary problems were not sufficient to endanger the completion of the work, domestic and personal problems, too, conspired against him. Having retired from his professorship, he had to move all of his books and papers out of his college office and into the garage he meant to use as a study in suburban Headington; he had to help Edith, who was becoming increasingly arthritic and prone to digestive ailments, around the house; he had grandchildren to visit and old friends (whose company he missed sorely now that he did not see them at work) to lunch with; and, overwhelmingly, he had letters and telephone calls from fans to answer, which he did faithfully. Even after Allen and Unwin offered to provide some secretarial help with the correspondence, Tolkien spent a great deal of his time considering and answering questions raised by readers. Finally, there was the problem of finding a suitable location for living in retirement.

In the later years of their marriage, the Tolkiens, free of responsibility for small children and of the necessity to watch pennies, had taken to vacationing in the middle-class resort town of Bournemouth, on the southern coast of England. Sometimes they went there simply for pleasure; sometimes as a relief for Edith from the strain of housekeeping. As a resort town, Bournemouth tended to be friendly, comfortable, and, above all, nonintellectual. It was, that is, precisely the opposite of Oxford in the 1930s. And Edith loved it.

When, in the late sixties, increasing infirmities of age made it clear that the Tolkiens could not remain in the Headington house, concern for Edith's preferences and happiness made Bournemouth seem like the logical place for relocation. So in 1968 they left the Oxford suburbs for a modern bungalow in the seacoast town. Here, though he missed Oxford and association with "men of my own kind,"[19] Tolkien and Edith lived a reasonably happy life until her death at the end of 1971.

In general, life was good at Bournemouth. Creature comforts were provided on a level that surpassed anything in Tolkien's previous life; his privacy was protected as Allen and Unwin carefully kept the address and telephone number confidential; and Edith was happy. Still, *The Silmarillion* did not take shape, and Tolkien began to fear that perhaps it never would.

At Edith's death, Merton College of Oxford University invited Tolkien to return as a resident honorary fellow. This meant he could live in a college-owned house, watched over by a scout (a kind of general college servant) and his wife. He received an honorary Doctorate of Letters from Oxford in 1972 and was made a Commander of the British Empire. And seemingly accepting the unlikelihood of ever finishing *The Silmarillion*, he agreed with his youngest son, Christopher, that should he die before the book was completed, Christopher would take up the task.

On Friday, September 1, 1973, while visiting friends in Bournemouth, Tolkien was taken to the hospital and diagnosed as suffering from an acute bleeding gastric ulcer. By Saturday, a complicating chest infection had developed, and in the early hours of Sunday morning, he died. He was buried in a cemetery on the outskirts of Oxford, Wolvercote, next to Edith.

Like his life, Tolkien's reputation sheds light on two important realms of human endeavor: the scholarly and the creative. His effect on his academic profession is, perhaps, articulated as well as could be by an anonymous obituary writer for the London *Times* who wrote, "During the years 1925–35 he was, more than any other single man, responsible for closing the old rift between 'literature' and 'philology' in English studies at Oxford and thus giving the existing school its characteristic temper."[20]

Taking a broader view, Tolkien's student, S. T. R. O d'Ardenne, said of him, "Tolkien belonged to that very rare class of linguists, now becoming extinct, who . . . could understand and recapture the glamour of 'the word.' 'In the beginning was the Word, and the Word was with God, and the Word was God.' "[21]

2

∿∿∿∿∿∿∿∿∿∿∿∿∿∿∿∿∿∿

The Quest as Fairy Tale:
The Hobbit

In 1937 Tolkien's first book, *The Hobbit,* appeared on the children's lists of Allen and Unwin. It was an immediate success as a children's book, receiving consistently good reviews, though it made no impression at all on the adult market. Like the fairy tales to which it is closely akin, it was thought to be appropriate only for the nursery, though many reviewers noted that the ideal reader of the adventures of Bilbo Baggins would have to be imaginative, intelligent, and an excellent reader.[1] In writing *The Hobbit,* Tolkien had reasonable success in doing what he attempted to do, but what he attempted to do was neither complex nor ambitious. The plot is simple and linear; the characters tend to be all good or all bad; and the central issue—the battle between good and evil—is clearly drawn and clearly resolved. That is, *The Hobbit* lacks complexity in conception, in design, and in execution. Its simplicity and its obviously having been written down to a naive audience make it far less interesting and much less an artistic achievement than *The Lord of the Rings,* though the two works share many themes and some characters.

Critics who feel driven to identify the stylistic qualities that mark *The Hobbit* as a children's book characteristically point to the avuncular asides that appear throughout the narrative. In such asides as,

"It was just at this moment that Bilbo suddenly discovered the weak point in his plan. Most likely you saw it some time ago and have been laughing at him; but I don't suppose you would have done half so well yourselves in his place," they argue, the narrator not only intrudes on his own story by stepping into the narrative frame and addressing the readers directly, he is also coy and talks down to his readers. This much is probably true, as Tolkien repudiated his narrative stance in *The Hobbit* within a very short time after it was published, saying, *The Hobbit* was written in what I should now regard as bad style, as if one were talking to children. There's nothing my children loathed more. They taught me a lesson. Anything that was in any way marked out in the *The Hobbit* as for children, instead of just for people, they disliked—instinctively. I did too, now that I think about it."[2] However, there are other less exceptionable practices in language use that as clearly mark *The Hobbit* as a book intended for the young or the naive reader. These are narrative characteristics which serve to illustrate for the reader how literature is to be read, that is, how details of section or description may be used as the basis for inference.

Take, for example, the problem of characterization. One learns early on in *The Hobbit* that qualities of character may be surmised by looking closely at the kind of language the character uses. So Bilbo's description of Gandalf's fireworks, "They used to go up like great lilies and snapdragons and laburnums of fire and hang in the twilight all evening," tells us something of the way his mind works. But the narrator feels obliged to help his reader draw that inference—"You will notice already that Mr. Baggins was not quite so prosy as he liked to believe."

Similarly, the narrator does not quite trust his reader to see or appreciate the significance of Bilbo's decision to go down the tunnel to the treasure trove of Smaug. Though the description of the rumble and throb of Smaug's snoring creates a sense of a hell fire waiting below, and though Bilbo's reluctance to enter the tunnel has been made clear, the narrator adds, "Going on from there was the bravest thing he ever did. The tremendous things that happened afterward were as nothing compared to it. He fought the real battle in the tunnel, alone, before he saw the danger that lay in wait." Now, there is nothing wrong with these descriptions or with the others like them throughout the book. They are not exactly condescending in tone, nor are they really stylistically inappropriate. But they assume a very naive reader, one incapable of drawing inferences or understanding symbolic meaning. They assume, that is, a child.

There are, as well, other language choices and attitudes that show Tolkien was writing *The Hobbit* for a young audience and was manipulating the language in appropriate ways for such a group. For example, the narrator assumes that the reader will not be able to find his way around in any organization more complicated than straight chronology. Thus he feels obliged to take his reader by the hand when he does anything sophisticated, such as using a flashback. So, when chapter 13 ends with Bilbo and the dwarves wondering what happened to Smaug, chapter 14 begins by answering the question: "Now if you wish, like the dwarves, to hear news of Smaug, you must go back again to the evening when he smashed the door and flew off in a rage, two days before." That is as tidy an example of steering a naive reader through a transition that makes use of a sophisticated narrative device as one can imagine.

It is then quite sure that *The Hobbit* is a children's book, in the sense that it was written with a childish or naive reader in mind. But it does not logically follow,

as many critics seem to assume, that the book is un-
worthy of critical attention. Though Tolkien later
repudiated the technique of *The Hobbit,* he could not
(and would not have wanted to) deny that the work
still reflects the workings of his remarkably fertile
mind, and that, though the themes are treated in such
a way as to be accessible to children, they have enough
significance and enough subtlety of development to
reward the attentive adult. Like other fairy tales, *The
Hobbit* is thematically concerned with the human situation, not simply with childish ones.

Hobbits, the avuncular narrator tells us, are little
people, about half our height. They have brown curly
hair on their heads and on their feet, though they do
not have beards. They are good-natured and socia-
ble, appreciating their food and their tobacco (which
they call pipe-weed) and preferring brightly colored
clothes, particularly vests. They are very shy outside
their own territory and, consequently, are almost
never seen by "the big folks," as they call us.
Whenever they hear one of the big folks coming, they
steal away silently through the fields and woods of the
Shire, the region of Middle-earth where they live.

The hobbit is Bilbo Baggins, who, as he is sitting
down to tea one day, hears adventure knocking at his
door. Thirteen dwarves, led by Thorin, son of
Thráin, King Under the Mountain, have decided to
return to the Lonely Mountain of their ancestors to
reclaim the treasure stolen from them by Smaug
the Dragon. For reasons Bilbo does not understand,
the wizard Gandalf has chosen him to accompany the
dwarves and to help them to recover the treasure. *The
Hobbit* is the story of Bilbo's adventures with the
dwarves, his role in recovering the treasure, and his
return to his comfortable hobbit hole.

Thematically, *The Hobbit* is primarily concerned
with increasing maturity.[3] As Bilbo travels with the

dwarves through adventures with trolls, goblins, and giant spiders, he changes from a frightened, passive, ineffectual lover of domestic comfort to a brave, realistic, active planner of events who is willing to take responsibility for himself and others.

After being almost eaten by trolls (who are luckily outsmarted by Gandalf), almost murdered by goblins, threatened by a strange underground creature called Gollum (from whose lair comes a magical ring that makes the wearer invisible), rescued by eagles, and captured by giant spiders and then by Wood-elves, the adventurers finally reach the Lonely Mountain. Here Bilbo asserts his leadership and finds the treasure, awakening the dragon's wrath in the process. When the rampaging dragon is killed by one of the men who live along the lake at the base of the mountain, the dwarves think their claim to the treasure is clear. However, men and elves soon appear to claim a share, and war threatens to break out. Bilbo steals the Arkenstone, the most famous and most beautiful gem of the hoard, and gives it to the men to use as a lever against Thorin's claim of the whole treasure. In doing so, he hopes to avert a disaster. His effort fails, however, and men, dwarves, and elves are saved from shedding one another's blood only by the attack upon all of them by the goblins and Wargs who wish to avenge the losses they suffered at the hands of Thorin and Company earlier.

When the battle is over, Bilbo knows the bitterness and joy of heroic involvement in life. He returns home, quite a new hobbit, both shunned and honored for his unusual involvement in adventures: "He took to writing poetry and visiting the elves; and though many shook their heads and touched their foreheads and said 'Poor old Baggins!' and though few believed any of his tales, he remained very happy to the end of his days, and those were extraordinarily long." One could hardly ask for a more classic fairy-tale ending.

Having said that *The Hobbit* is a book much akin to a fairy tale, it would perhaps be a good idea to consider that statement for a moment: What are the characteristics associated with fairy tales? Fairy tales are stories that take place in a secondary world—a world in which nature is alive in a nearly human way, and the laws that govern man and nature are not the same as those of the world we occupy. Thus, in the world of a fairy tale, animals may talk, magic may happen, people may come back to life, or live for extraordinarily long expanses of time. The heroes of fairy tales tend to be the small and the weak —youngest brothers or sisters, for example, or people who are thought to be dullards. But they have virtues that allow them to overcome the strong and the powerful—a good nature, or a streak of kindness, or an amazing cunning quickness. In fairy tales, good and evil tend to be presented in black and white, although the distinction is more likely to be made on the basis of what the hero needs psychologically than what the laws of religion or property teach us. For example, in "Jack the Giant Killer," it is far more important to Jack's story that he outsmart the giant and his wife than that the rights of property be respected, that is, that the giant retain possession of his golden harp. The giant is clearly bad because he tries to keep Jack from existing as an individual (by eating him), and in the eyes of the fairy tale that is a more important crime than Jack's theft, which is part of his growing up.

By contrast, the hero of myth or legend tends to be a godlike being, if not in fact a god. Though we may admire such a hero and may long to be like him, we know we cannot, simply because he is too far above us. The argument is essentially the same one used to

explain why Christianity finds it necessary to con-
ceive of a God that is both god and man: If his followers are to emulate him, Christ must be within the
realm of possible emulation, as a god is not.

Finally, a fairy tale tends to have a simple linear
structure—its episodes tend to be arranged in the
order in which they occur in time. In recounting the
episodes the teller usually makes use of repetition of
incidents, so that a character might have three wishes
or three tasks or three adventures. In shorter tales
the repetition may occur in the speech or in the descriptions, as in " 'Little pig, little pig, let me come in.'
'Not by the hair of your chinny, chin chin.' "

The Hobbit, Tolkien's first published work of fantasy, bears a strong resemblance to the fairy tale,
particularly in its structure, its interest in the idea of
heroism, and its attention to the opposition between
good and evil. Structurally, *The Hobbit* is neat and
tidy, almost elegant. As its subtitle, "There and Back
Again," suggests, the underlying metaphor is the
journey, and although the trip out occupies most of
the space of the book, the trip back is equally important. Bilbo's journey from the Shire, where he is
staid, passive, and bland, to the Lonely Mountain,
where he is resourceful, active, and assertive, marks a
shift in his character as much as in his geographical
location. As is always the case with literary journeys,
Bilbo can not exactly go home again. Though the
physical journey may end where it began, the
psychological journey does not simply retrace its
steps. What Bilbo gains in maturity and in understanding of his world will, the book promises, last far
beyond the end of his journey.

Although the structure of *The Hobbit* is basically
circular, Bilbo's development is linear. When the author diverges from this strategy, he throws up road
signs, as when he guides us through the flashback at

the beginning of chapter 14. Bilbo's growth from childish passivity to mature involvement both proceeds and is recounted in a straight line. Besides having the virtue of simplicity, Tolkien's narrative strategy helps to make clear the stages of Bilbo's progress by showing us how Bilbo's own attitudes and those of his antagonists change from episode to episode.

In the opening pages, Bilbo and his situation are painted in broadly comic strokes. Gandalf's power and control are contrasted with Bilbo's youth as suggested by his bright green door—the color of the newness of spring—and his inability to resist being manipulated. Despite Bilbo's repeated assertions, "No adventures wanted here, thank you," Gandalf places a sign on the door that says, "Burglar wants a good job, plenty of Excitement and reasonable Reward." When the dwarves arrive, Bilbo is too polite to turn them away; when they almost leave without him, and he has settled down to a second breakfast and a nice cup of tea, Gandalf shoos him out the door without his pipe or even so much as a pocket-handkerchief. From this ignominious beginning Bilbo consistently progresses until he is making decisions that affect the fates of several races—dwarves, elves, and men.

It is true that Bilbo has to be rescued by Gandalf from Bert, Tom, and William, the trolls who capture the thirteen dwarves and the one hobbit before Gandalf tricks them into staying outside until the sun comes up and turns them into stone. And it is also true that without Gandalf neither Bilbo nor the dwarves would have escaped from the goblins who carried them deep inside the Misty Mountains. But it is equally true that without Bilbo's warning, Gandalf would not have been free to help them escape from the goblins' cave. More important, it is true that once

Bilbo has escaped from the goblins, who want to kill him, and from Gollum, who wants to eat him, he is quite capable of deciding that if his friends are still inside the terrifying caverns of the mountain, he must return to try to free them. He has to decide what to do, and his decision, though he is not called upon to act on it, is the right one.

In the early episodes of the story Bilbo's maturity increases in a way that lets him move from concern for himself only to concern for a small group—his friends. In the later episodes his moral base becomes yet broader, so that by the final chapters, Bilbo is capable of stealing the Arkenstone, the Heart of the Mountain and a gem that he covets greatly (as does everyone who sees it), and then of giving it to Bard, Lord of Dale, in an attempt to prevent a war between the dwarves and men. That he failed in this noble attempt is less important than that it was his own idea and he tried it.

One is never completely free of fate in the world of *The Hobbit*. Prophecies abound and they come true, nonetheless so because Bilbo and Gandalf are involved with them. But Bilbo will never again be entirely subject to fate either, as he now knows that he is capable of having adventures. The part of Bilbo that can kill a giant spider, engineer an escape from the Wood-elves' cavern, and steal down a dark tunnel toward a sleeping dragon cannot be driven back into his unconscious again. Like the sword over the fireplace and the chain mail in the front hall of Bag End, Bilbo's new-found maturity is something to keep and cherish.

We can see, then, that Bilbo steadily increases in maturity and responsibility throughout the story. It is not just Bilbo's character changing that seems so right in this linear structure of episodes. Tolkien has also taken pains to give Bilbo opponents who become consistently more elemental, that is, less human and more nearly forces of nature. In doing so he has used the principle of repetition, particularly in developing a series of three descents into the underworld.

The first is the descent in the goblins' cave, in which Bilbo encounters Gollum, whose greed is of the simplest physical and sensual kind—he wants food. Though he has long lived under the mountain, Gollum once lived in Middle-earth, paddled in a river, taught his grandmother to suck eggs, and loved to see the sun shine on the daisies. However, in the course of his life under the mountain, Gollum's simple sensual greed has become more dangerous: "Goblins . . . he just throttled from behind."

The second is the descent into the caverns of the King of the Wood-elves. Wood-elves, says the narrator, are not really wicked. They have some magical powers, though not as strong as the powers of the High Elves who went to Faerie in the West. The Elf-King's greed is for "silver and white gems." The Wood-elves are greater foes than Gollum because they are themselves magic rather than simply having possession of a magical device, so they cannot be disarmed as Gollum was, and because their greed is not mindlessly physical, but directed toward the abstract beautiful—in short, it is spiritual. Faith and pity (with a good dollop of courage) were sufficient to escape from Gollum, but to engineer the escape of Thorin and Company from the halls of the Wood-elf king requires good sense and intelligence as well. As Gollum is by his own choice a little below the human, the Wood-elves are a little above it. They are not more dangerous physically than Gollum, but they are more challenging opponents.

The third is the journey to the heart of the Lonely Mountain and the hoard of Smaug. Bilbo's dragon, though treated with a comic touch now and then, is a personification of simple greed and the malice that accompanies it. Smaug, with his diamond waistcoat (a parody of Bilbo's taste for colorful clothes), and his bed heaped with gold and jewels represents a greed that far exceeds mere physical appetite or aesthetic pleasure. At the discovery of the loss of his cup, stolen by Bilbo, Smaug flies into a rage—"the sort of rage that is only seen when rich folk that have more than they can enjoy suddenly lose something that they have long had but have never before used or wanted." Smaug's rage and greed, then, exist separately from Bilbo and the cup. He is a representative of a general evil—a less human, less understandable, less limited evil than Gollum or the Wood-elves.

As there is a progression in the kind and quality of Bilbo's opponents, there is also a progression in the trials he must undergo in order to return from each of his journeys underground. In his first two adventures underground, he discovers and takes possession of treasures for himself—first the sword, which he takes from the trolls' cave and which has an elvish blade (i.e., is a hero's weapon) and then the ring, which is magical, too, though not elvish. The sword's phallic associations and its masculine suggestions of aggression combine with its elvish nature (goodness) to connote an active opposition to the forces of evil, while the ring, a symbol of the feminine, of wholeness, perfection, and the eternal suggests a more passive but equally strong commitment to the good, especially as it is associated with Bilbo's pity for Gollum and his decision to make a leap of faith in the dark rather than to rely on his sword to escape from under the mountain. With the sword and the ring together, Bilbo possesses and balances the two sides of the human—the aggressive and the passive, the physical and the spiritual, the male and the female.

And with the help of the sword and the ring he literally overcomes the darkness and finds the light at the end of the tunnel.

In outsmarting the Wood-elves and helping Thorin and Company to escape by water, Bilbo advances from saving himself to saving a select group—the dwarves he knows and who know him. The passage of Bilbo and the company of dwarves through the narrow passage that leads from the caverns of the Elf-King to the domain of the Lakemen is reminiscent of the birth process and hence of the rebirth process. Certainly it is true that Bilbo is reborn in the eyes of the dwarves—Thorin begins to think of him as "the remarkable Mr. Baggins," and as for everyone else, "they all trusted Bilbo. Just what Gandalf had said would happen, you see."

As Bilbo's actions in the caverns of the Wood-elves represent one step in a progression, his willingness to descend into the home of Smaug represents another. The escape from the Wood-elves is a trial by water, but the escape from Smaug is a trial by fire as Bilbo is pursued up the passageway by the dragon's hot breath. As the dragon is a more serious threat than the Wood-elves, Bilbo's intentions in the final episode are more heroic than earlier. Where he had been committed to saving himself and those to whom he had a personal attachment, he is, in the Smaug episode, acting in what he takes to be the best interest of humankind. That is, from a parochial view it may be that he has betrayed Thorin and Company, but from a broader view he is acting in what he thinks are the best interests of all civilized beings. So the trial by fire is a greater trial than that by darkness or by water, and as such it comes in response to a greater effort and a more heroic intent.

So far we have seen that, rather than being a simple and episodic little adventure story, *The Hobbit* is a carefully structured tale that uses a principle of progression (of journeys to the underworld, of the quality of opponents) to create a sense of working toward a climax. We have also seen that the journey motif, the "There and Back Again" part of the story, encloses the two progressions in a circular structure which in turn gives the story a sense of completion.

Within the tidy circular structure, Tolkien develops two major and universal themes, both as accessible to children as they are to adults: the nature of heroism in a comic world and the conflict between good and evil. These are typical fairy-tale themes; however, Tolkien's fairy tale is distinguished from most others by the complexity he accords to these issues and by the way he combines them with a far less common theme in children's books, the power of language.

A distinctive part of Tolkien's fiction is his vision of what it means to be a hero and what is the nature of heroism. His concern with heroism in *The Hobbit* is limited in scope to a kind of hero we may call low mimetic—the hero who is no better than we are, neither in kind nor in degree. And that hero is, of course, Bilbo Baggins. From the first scenes of the book, Bilbo's limitations, his differences from the high-mimetic heroes of myth who are either gods or godlike men, very different from us, are clear. Bilbo is "very respectable," which means he "never had any adventures or did anything unexpected." Gandalf, the wizard, whose machinations set Bilbo in motion, understands clearly that Bilbo is not a mythic hero, and he understands that mythic heroes are high mimetic, but as he points out to the dwarves, "I tried to find one; but warriors are busy fighting one another in distant lands, and in this neighborhood heroes are scarce, or simply not to be found." As in that most typical of British fairy tales, "Jack the Giant

Killer," the best possibility for heroism in the Shire is to be found in a burglar.

Bilbo Baggins, then, has possibilities. He is, for example, the son of "the fabulous Belladonna Took" and may through her be descended from fairies. As a result, there is something more to Bilbo, "something that only [waits] for a chance to come out." Furthermore, like many low-mimetic heroes, Bilbo has a taste for real heroes of the high-mimetic kind—he loves "wonderful tales . . . about dragons and goblins and giants and the rescue of princesses and the unexpected luck of widow's sons." That is, even the least likely looking hobbit has by inheritance and imagination some heroic possibilities.

Just as Bilbo's sense of his own possibilities as a hero increases throughout the story, so does the seriousness of his motives. His first adventure, in which he and all the company are captured by trolls, is strictly a comic event. Bilbo is depicted as a being of limited experience, one whose sheltered life keeps him from understanding the ways of the world, particularly the part of the world where people "have seldom even heard of the King," that is, where the rules differ from those of the Shire. Thus, his naivete, his lack of competence, and his taste for animal comforts, which he shares with the dwarves and the reader, are all roundly ridiculed.

As the book progresses, however, Bilbo's ridiculousness is tempered with quite another quality. By the time he is captured and escapes from the goblins and from Gollum, his determination to return to the goblin caverns and search for his friends has the effect of connecting him with two significant high-mimetic heroes: Christ and Gandalf. The connection with Christ is tenuous but real, resulting from the conjunction of the language of the passage with the New Testament "greater love hath no man than this:

that he lay down his life for his friend," as Tolkien writes, "He wondered whether he ought not, now he had the magic ring, to go back into the horrible, horrible tunnels and look for his friends." The connection with Gandalf is less tenuous; it results from Bilbo's willingness to assume the role of shepherd that Gandalf has portrayed so far and is trying to persuade the dwarves to help him portray again: "Gandalf was saying that they could not possibly go on with their journey leaving Mr. Baggins in the hands of the goblins without trying to find out if he was alive or dead, and without trying to rescue him."

"After all he is my friend," said the wizard, "and not a bad little chap." Gandalf and Bilbo, the high-mimetic and low-mimetic heroes, sharing a willingness to return to the "horrible, horrible, tunnels" to save their friends, are set apart from the dwarves, who are ruled by their own fears: "If we have got to go back now into those abominable tunnels to look for him, then drat him, I say." Dwarves are not, as the narrator says later, bad people, but they are not heroes.

Once Bilbo and Gandalf are set up as representing the low-mimetic and high-mimetic sides of the hero, Gandalf may leave to attend to "some pressing business away south." His concern with and responsibility for the world beyond, foreshadowed early in his meeting Thorin's father in the dungeons of the Necromancer and in his decision not to let the Wargs "have it all their own way," looks forward to his return in time for the Battle of the Five Armies with its wider implications for Middle-earth.

Gandalf leaves Thorin and Company with a series of warnings that sound very like Christian's exhortations to himself in *Pilgrim's Progress:* "We may meet again before this is all over and then again we may not. That depends on your luck and on your courage and sense." That is, not everything is foreordained. Both God and man have a hand in shaping all that happens: God through the medium of grace, which Tolkien calls "luck," and man through his physical and rational excellences, bravery and sense, which, at their best, represent the God-like in man.

That Gandalf is only a hero of a higher order or perhaps a messenger of God is suggested by his own limitations—he can be afraid, though he is a wizard and, he admits, his success in bringing the troop through the mountains has depended upon the same forces on which they must rely—"good management and good luck."

While Gandalf, the high-mimetic hero, is a loner, one particularly important quality in Bilbo's heroism as it develops in the episodes before Thorin and Company reach the city of Esgaroth upon the long lake is its essential socialness. From the moment Bilbo bursts out of his house without his pipe or his pipe-weed, or even a pocket-handkerchief, his movement has always been *toward* the dwarves. Separated from them by Wood-elves, he always moves toward the company of the adventurers. The paradox is that although he always moves *toward,* Bilbo is also always gaining in confidence, competence, and character —all the qualities that lead to self-sufficiency. By the time the dwarves escape from the caverns of the Wood-elves, Bilbo is clearly the leader, and even Thorin must agree to follow him. In doing what he must do to remain a part of the group, Bilbo takes responsibility for it; taking responsibility makes him a leader and sets him apart, isolates him from the group, as illustrated in the descriptions of the escape from the caverns of the Wood-elves: "He was in the dark tunnel, floating in icy water, all alone—for you cannot count friends that are all packed up in barrels."

By the time of the escape from the Wood-elves, Bilbo has developed as far as is possible in the direction of his small society. Yet the end of the quest has not been achieved. The possibilities for continuing are two: Bilbo may stop in his development (as Tom Sawyer does) and simply lead the dwarves to the treasure, or he may continue to develop in some way that parallels the continuation of the quest. The first possibility is unlikely, for it would reduce the importance of the final episode to a simple working out of plot. The tale would become mere episodic adventure instead of a unified quest. But if Bilbo is to continue to develop, which direction must he take? The answer is provided in Gandalf's example: As Gandalf's "some pressing business away south" suggests a responsibility to the wider world beyond the company, Bilbo eventually finds that he has a wider responsibility, too—to the men of Esgaroth, to the king of the Wood-elves, to the Five Armies. And yet, Thorin and Company cannot be utterly deserted, for they are a part of that wider world too.

The movement of Bilbo away from the society of Thorin and Company is evident as soon as the party leaves Esgaroth for the Lonely Mountain—and it is here that the sense of making Bilbo a hobbit rather than another dwarf or an elf becomes clear—he is with the company but not of them. Though the company finds the door in the mountain without too much delay, they are quite unable to guess its secret until a day when "the dwarves all went wandering off in various directions . . . . All day Bilbo sat gloomily in the grassy bay gazing at the stone, or out west through the narrow opening." Here the real movement of Bilbo away from the company begins, and it begins in contemplation of the west—the source of wisdom and creativity, though also the symbol of the end.

Tolkien uses structural repetition to demonstrate Bilbo's growth in this episode. Once the door is opened and Bilbo is in the tunnel, the situation is very like that following the escape from the goblins' tunnel when Bilbo was pursued by Gollum: He accepts his duty to do for the dwarves, even though he cannot (and does not) hope that the dwarves will do for him:

> The most that can be said for the dwarves is this: they intended to pay Bilbo really handsomely for his services; they had brought him to do a nasty job for them, and they did not mind the little fellow doing it if he would; but they would all have done their best to get him out of trouble, if he got into it, as they did in the case of the trolls at the beginning of their adventures before they had any reason for being grateful to him. There it is: dwarves are not heroes, but calculating folk with a great idea of the value of money; some are tricky and treacherous and pretty bad lots; some are not, but are decent enough people like Thorin and Company, if you don't expect too much.

There are two important suggestions about Tolkien's view of the nature of heroism in this passage. First, it suggests that heroism is active rather than reactive, because Thorin and Company are steady and brave in rescuing friends in need, as Thorin's reaction when Smaug leaves his den will show. But Bilbo must be the initiator of action, not just a reactor. And he becomes an initiator when he steps into the tunnel and begins, for the first time, to move out away from the company and toward the wide world. As was true when he escaped from the goblins, his most heroic act in this scene is a pyschological one: Once out of the horrible goblin caves, Bilbo had decided to go back inside to search for his companions if necessary. Here, once inside the tunnel, Bilbo makes another heroic decision—to keep going further despite the agonizing fear he feels when he hears Smaug's snoring and sees his red glow.

This is an important step for Bilbo, because it transforms him. Smaug's dream, prophetic as it is, features no burglars and no grocers. Instead, it is "an uneasy dream (in which a warrior, altogether insignificant in size, but provided with a bitter sword and great courage, figured most unpleasantly)." In deciding to go on alone, Bilbo becomes the warrior that Gandalf was looking for, and Smaug's dream of a warrior foreshadows the gift of the mithril mail Thorin will give Bilbo in recognition of his bravery.

In the encounter with Smaug, the confrontation with the men of Dale, and the Battle of the Five Armies, Bilbo demonstrates the final defining quality of his low-mimetic heroism, the ability to go on when there is no hope. Whether the issue is recovering the treasure by getting rid of Smaug ("Personally, I have no hopes at all . . ."), or rescuing dwarves from Wood-elves ("he was not as hopeful as they were"), Bilbo's hopelessness is always short-lived and gives way to hope that springs from plans and action. Though Bilbo's states of hopelessness never last as long as Frodo's will in *The Lord of the Rings,* Tolkien sounds the first notes of the theme in *The Hobbit.*

By the closing chapters of the story, the reader has long understood that Bilbo's capacity for physical bravery is far greater than he thought, so we are not surprised when, in the Battle of the Five Armies, he draws his sword to stand with the Elvenking. But the side of heroism Bilbo reveals in giving up the Arkenstone, the sacrificial act that repudiates the heart of the mountain and the heart of Thorin, is a binding force: It draws men to it and binds them. Bilbo's giving up the Arkenstone, that is, his expressing a commitment to the wider world that comes before his commitment to Thorin and Company, unites him not only with Gandalf but also with the high-mimetic hero, Bard.

Bard, as the high-mimetic hero Bilbo is not, foreshadows the kind of heroism that will be represented by Aragorn, the king of men, in *The Lord of the Rings*. He is a man of heroic stature, the descendant of kings, and the protector of his people. Thus he is the kind of hero who may be expected to slay dragons, a traditional high-mimetic heroic feat. Furthermore, like Aragorn, Bard is a healer. After Smaug's destruction of Esgaroth, he is quick "to help in the ordering of the camps and in the care of the sick and the wounded," and when he approaches Thorin to demand a portion of the treasure, he asks for it in the name of justice, but also in the name of mercy.

High-mimetic heroism, then, of the kind demonstrated by warrior kings and other men or demigods of heroic proportions appears in *The Hobbit* not so much as a vision of heroism in which Tolkien is particularly interested at this time, but as a background against which the quality of Bilbo's heroism (and by implication, the heroism of which the reader is capable) may be more clearly seen. The viewing of Bilbo's deeds against the assumptions about heroes underlying the heroism of Gandalf and Bard illustrates clearly that the ordinary man, though he cannot work magic or kill dragons, can do what a hero does: He can save us. It also illustrates that the qualities of the low-mimetic hero need not be great strength or great wisdom, but a kind heart, a hopeful disposition, and a love of his fellow beings. As Gandalf reminds Bilbo at the end of the story, "You are a very fine person, Mr. Baggins, and I am fond of you; but you are only quite a little fellow in a wide world after all." Indeed, suggests Tolkien, so are we all.

While the nature of heroism is the major theme

of *The Hobbit,* a closely allied theme is concerned with
the nature of good and evil: Many of the central
episodes and characters of *The Hobbit* reflect
Tolkien's thinking about the origin and nature of
good and evil. A central point of differentiation in his
vision has to do with the impulse for acquisition.

At home in the Shire Bilbo is, as an extension of
being "respectable," comfortable, and thus acquisitive. His hobbit-hole is distinguished by well-stocked
pantries, "(lots of these,)" and equally well-stocked
wardrobes, "(he had whole rooms devoted to
clothes)." Like nearly everyone else in Middle-earth,
he is always deeply concerned with what he puts in his
mouth—he finds a pipe very soothing and satisfying,
and he finds a little something to eat or drink even
more so. As a respectable domestic character, he is
not unconscious of the concepts of duty and sacrifice,
but the concepts have assumed some curious forms.
When the dwarves begin to arrive at his hole, for
example, "He had a horrible thought that the cakes
might run short, and then he—as the host: he knew
his duty and stuck to it however painful—he might
have to go without." Nothing unique; nothing even
exceptional; certainly nothing dangerous in itself.
But also certainly something that foreshadows trouble to come.

In keeping with the embryonic conception of evil
in *The Hobbit,* the source of Bilbo's trouble with the
trolls is the impulse for acquisition. And, in Bilbo's
case that impulse is usually expressed in terms of
sensory comfort. He has no business with trolls, and
the whole episode results from an unnecessary devo-
tion (both his and the dwarves') to fire and food. In
fact, the acquisitive motive is made clear by Bilbo's
decision to pick the pocket of one of the trolls. Like
the hen and the harp of "Jack the Giant Killer," however, the troll's purse betrays the burglar to its owner,

who, like the giant, proposes to "acquire" the thief in his own way, i.e., to eat the "burrahobbit."

By the time of the second episode of the adventure, the capture by goblins and the meeting with Gollum, Bilbo is ready to take a more active part in saving the company. It is he who warns them and gives Gandalf the opportunity to escape capture by the goblins by giving "as loud a yell as a hobbit can give, which is surprising for their size." Bilbo's contribution here is an important one because until now he has had very little control over his life or his actions. The first scenes, frustrating for Bilbo (though richly comic for the reader), show him utterly at the mercy of Gandalf. Gandalf determines to send him on an adventure; Gandalf sends the dwarves to Bilbo's house; and when it appears that Bilbo will miss the whole enterprise in the interest of doing breakfast dishes for fourteen, Gandalf sends him off on the run, without so much as a pocket-handkerchief. Bilbo is entirely subject, that is, to predetermination as represented by Gandalf. But in warning Gandalf in time and so contributing to his own rescue and the encounter with Gollum, Bilbo brings free will and grace into the picture.

Separated from Gandalf and the dwarves in the goblin caves, Bilbo wakes from unconsciousness into a new state of consciousness. Though for "a long while" he thinks of frying eggs and bacon in his own kitchen (that is, of security, of absorbing things into himself), he soon perceives that the nature of his world has changed. The quality of that change is reflected in his lack of matches (doing nothing but having a smoke is no longer a choice available to him) and, more important, in his rediscovery of his sword, taking action in the world is possible. Thus his recognition that to go forward is the only choice is a moral and psychological insight as well as a pragmatic one.

Bilbo's encounter with Gollum is an example of the journey to the underworld archetype, the mythic journey of the hero to the land of the dead where he acquires some knowledge or some talisman that will help him to achieve his earthly quest, though Tolkien introduces some curious comic inversions into the archetype as, for example, having Gollum guard the exit rather than the entrance, and having Bilbo find the talisman without knowing he is looking for it.

Several important changes occur in Bilbo as a result of his having found that going forward is the only thing to do. He is revealed to have grace; he is revealed to have charity (pity); he is brought to the state of psychic/symbolic wholeness that lets him move into the area where low-mimetic and high-mimetic heroism overlap.

Grace is a divine influence which operates in men to regenerate and sanctify, to inspire virtuous impulses, and to impart strength to endure trial and resist temptation. Because its source is divine, grace is beyond the control of man, as Bilbo's winning the riddle game results from forces beyond his control, which the author calls "luck." The notion that grace is a serious force in the Gollum episode is strengthened by the eschatological nature of the scene. The journey to the underworld is archetypally a journey to the land of the dead, and Gollum's riddles, reflecting his life under the mountain, focus steadily on the end of things:

> It cannot be seen, cannot be felt,
> Cannot be heard, cannot be smelt.
> It lies behind stars and under hills,
>   And empty holes it fills.
> It comes first and follows after,
>   *Ends life, kills laughter.*
>   Ans. Dark

Alive without breath,
As cold as death,
Never thirsty, ever drinking,
All in mail never clinking.

Ans. Fish

This thing all things devours:
Birds, beasts, trees, flowers;
Gnaws iron, bites steels;
Grinds hard stones to meal;
Slays kings, *ruins* town,
And beats high mountain down.

Ans. Time*

And what saves Bilbo from the threat of death is not his talent for riddling, which is surely mediocre, but "pure luck," both in answering Gollum's riddle and in asking a question beyond Gollum's ability to answer. And even before that, his luck is in finding the ring and in slipping the ring on, and then falling down in the tunnel when Gollum is chasing him. The terminology Tolkien uses in the riddling scene shows the real nature of the force that saves Bilbo. The time riddle evokes the idea of the end—total destruction of all things without hope of renewal. And when Bilbo squeals "Time! Time!" the narrator comments, "Bilbo was saved by pure luck." In addition, Bilbo several times refers to himself as "lost" and wanting to get "unlost." But to get "unlost," or saved, requires more than grace. It requires, in addition, charity and faith, and the interrelation between the two. Grace, or luck, continues to play an important part as Bilbo and Gollum race up the tunnel. It is grace or luck that the ring slips on Bilbo's finger at the right moment and that he falls in the tunnel so that Gollum can pass him. But it is charity (Tolkien calls it pity) that keeps Bilbo from killing Gollum, that lets him appreciate

*Author italics.

the horror of being without grace, of living "endless unmarked days without light or hope of betterment." And it is faith combined with grace and charity that finally propels him past Gollum. The pity he feels for Gollum calls up "a new strength and resolve," which lets Bilbo make the leap of faith: "No great leap for a man, but a leap in the dark [in which Bilbo] only just missed cracking his skull on the low arch of the passage."

Neither grace nor faith nor charity nor free will is sufficient by itself—they are all working together to produce a Bilbo reborn as a hero with heroic potential. Bilbo's wholeness is symbolized in his conscious possession of the ring (a circle symbolizing the feminine spiritual) and the sword (symbolizing the male aggressive).

The significance to Bilbo's development as a hero of the experience with the goblins at the root of the mountain is apparent almost immediately as Bilbo, free and wandering on the edge of the Land Beyond, realizes that he has a responsibility to search for his company: "He wondered whether he ought not, now he had the magic ring, to go back into the horrible, horrible tunnels and look for his friends. He had just made up his mind that it was his duty, that he must turn back—and very miserable he felt about it—when he heard voices." Two important things happen in these quick sentences: 1. For the second time, Tolkien uses the word *duty* in reference to Bilbo, but this time the duty—to risk his life for his friends—is worthy of the name in a way that the trivial going without cakes was not; 2. In recognizing his duty and, more important, in resolving to do it, Bilbo makes the psychological commitment that makes him a real hero even though he is not required to express that commitment in action just yet. Still, the commitment itself is a mental event of great importance.

The willingness to sacrifice oneself cannot result from thoughtlessness; it is a moral decision and a difficult one. It is also a meaningless decision if no fear or danger enters into it (that is, if there is no real danger to oneself). Critics who argue that Gandalf's status as a hero is undercut by the narrator's observation that Gandalf was afraid of the goblins "wizard though he was" are working from a curiously perverted idea of heroism. What is important is not that Gandalf is frightened, but that his fright does not diminish his heroic stature—he still responds as if to protect the others as best he can though the situation seems hopeless: "Gandalf climbed to the top of his tree. The sudden splendor flashed from his wand like lightning, as he got ready to spring down from on high right among the spears of the goblins. That would have been the end of him, though he would probably have killed many of them as he came hurtling down like a thunderbolt. But he never leaped." It is perhaps appropriate to note here that, contrary to some critical opinion, Gandalf's self-sacrificial state of mind is not simply limited in implication to the well-being of Thorin and Company. Though it is not until the closing pages of the book that Gandalf reminds Bilbo of the interconnections in the world, the scene in which the troop are all treed by the Wargs and goblins sounds the theme very early. The appearance of Thorin and Company in the glade that is the meeting place of the Wargs has immediate and serious repercussions in the lives of many "bold," "brave and well-armed" woodsmen who are taming the wild and "making their way back into it from the South." The threat to these people from the Wargs and Goblins is as serious as the threat to Thorin and Company, for "If their plan had been carried out, there would have been none left there next day; all would have been killed except the few the goblins kept from the wolves and carried back as prisoners to

their caves." But Gandalf, whose heroic responsibilities are wider than Thorin and Company, "was
not going to let them have it all their own way, though
he could not do very much stuck up in a tall tree with
wolves all around on the ground below."

Once Gandalf leaves and Bilbo and the dwarves
enter Mirkwood, Bilbo becomes, for all practical
purposes, the leader of the band. It is he who sees
most clearly in the gloom, and it is he who is "light"
enough to ascend to the top of the trees, though no
vision of a heavenly city rewards him. More important, to Bilbo falls the task of saving the dwarves from
the giant spiders and from the Wood-elves.

In saving Thorin and Company from the giant
spiders, Bilbo reenacts Gandalf's rescue of the whole
group from the trolls. The complication in both incidents is that in searching for something to eat (to
absorb, internalize, "swallow up"), is that one runs the
danger of being eaten by somebody else. This danger
is greater as the party becomes more "consumed" by
its passion—finding the treasure. But before Bilbo
can save the dwarves, he must save himself, and his
doing so is one of the most important episodes in his
development. Characteristically, he falls asleep,
"thinking of his far-distant hobbit-hole with its beautiful pantries." Wish-fulfillment fantasies are a
dangerous indulgence for one whose instructions are
to trust to luck, bravery, and sense, and this one
almost does for Bilbo. But unlike Bombur, Bilbo can
exchange his fantasy for action when the time comes,
although he for a moment forgets his best weapon
—his sword—and it is by luck that he awakes in time
to use it.

The structure of Bilbo's defeat of the giant spiders is surely that of the archetypal romance: The
hero, alone in a strange and threatening environ-
ment, encounters and slays a monstrous opponent.

The narrator tells us that, "Somehow, the killing of the giant spider, all alone by himself in the dark without the help of the wizard of the dwarves or of anyone else, made a great difference to Mr. Baggins," but he doesn't say exactly what kind of change. However, he shows what kind of change by showing Bilbo taking one more step in imitation of high-mimetic herohood—he has Bilbo name his sword: "I will give you a name," he said to it, "and I shall call you *Sting*." Aside from the mythoreligious echoes contained in it, Bilbo's proclamation and the actual naming of the weapon allies him once again with Gandalf (and Thorin Oakenshield), both of whom carry named swords.

Occurring spontaneously and without any reference to the ring, Bilbo's success in overcoming his own giant spider most of all illustrates his bravery and his luck. But Gandalf has warned that luck, bravery, and sense would be needed, and the twin rescues of the dwarves, first from the spiders and then from the Wood-elves, are chances for Bilbo to use his sense.

Finding the dwarves hanging in the trees like so many sides of beef, Bilbo turns Gandalf's troll-baiting trick to good use, an event which further parallels him with Gandalf. However, there is a mixture of motive in Bilbo's heroics that we never see in Gandalf. That is, not only does Bilbo wish to do what he can to save his friends (that much the two of them share), he also regards them as a necessary component of his own being in a very immediate and social way. His first words after the ritual naming of the sword are a lament for his isolation from his friends: "What a mess we are in now! We! I only wish it was we: it is horrible being all alone." The same attitude of psychological vulnerability is struck when the dwarves are captured by the Wood-elves: "He did not wish to desert the dwarves, and indeed he did not know where in the world to go without them."

The Hobbit, like traditional fairy tales, is less concerned with the broad conflict between good and evil
than with the personal growth of the hero. At the
same time, the rudiments of Tolkien's visions of good
and evil, while not central, are clearly and consistently depicted in the actions and motives of Bilbo
and those he encounters in his adventures. Fantasy, it
has been said, reenacts the process of creation, and in
The Hobbit the issues of good and evil are inextricably
bound up with creativity, especially the creation of
beauty. In some ways, this connection has a Platonic
ring to it—those who are evil are frightening or ugly
in appearance. For example, the trolls on the moun-
tainside have "heavy faces" and speak like working-
class urban Englishmen—their language "was not
drawing room at all," and their manners are
worse—they jog one another's elbows, wipe their
mouths on their sleeves, and lose their tempers often
and violently.

Good, on the other hand, is expressed as a kind
of Inklings society—composed of creative and merry
males, the good society values hospitable conviviality
(as in the reception Beorn gives the company and the
singing of the elves in Rivendell). Indeed, there as in
The Lord of the Rings, most value accrues to the elves
whose virtue and superiority Bilbo recognizes even
though the Wood-elves had been opponents of Thorin and Company.

"The dreadful language of the Wargs" sounds so
dreadful because it is used to talk about "cruel and
wicked things." As the Wargs' language suggests, if
evil beings do create anything (and most of them do
not) it will not be beautiful. The goblins, for example,
"are cruel, wicked, and badhearted. They make no
beautiful things, but they make many clever ones."
They have as much engineering skill as dwarves, but

they are "untidy and dirty" and their taste runs to tools and instruments of torture, so their caves and tunnels are dark and rough, while the dwarf halls under the mountain are spacious, smooth, and airy. Yet the real heart of evil is not in the creation of the ugly or the wicked but in the destruction of the beautiful and the good. Dragons are evil because they do not create or enjoy; they only hoard. Further, in their "cruel" wickedness, they destroy both man-made accomplishments (the towns of Dale and Esgaroth) and natural beauty (the banks of the bright River Running and the side of the Lonely Mountain).

For Bilbo to be made an Elf-friend, then, is a final sign of his growth and entrance into the world of the creative and the good. And to be an Elf-friend seems to mean to have a creative vision (for Bilbo begins to compose poetry and to write his memoirs, which will become part of the famous Red Book of Westmarch). He has the friendship of elves and the honor of dwarves, but most important, he has self-knowledge, and that is the greatest good of this heroic fairy-story.

In order to complete his development as an Elf-friend, Bilbo must move beyond his being as a hero and beyond his part in the battle between good and evil to become a third being: a user of language. Tolkien's fascination with languages, such an important element in the imaginative world of *The Lord of the Rings* and *The Silmarillion,* is also apparent in *The Hobbit.* Here, however, as is appropriate to his comic intent, he is not above making use of various forms of wordplay for the amusement of his young audience. Thus puns and riddles abound, with references to proverbs, only slightly unfamiliar, sprinkled about liberally. One might also rank among the uses of language likely to be most appreciated by children

the secret language syndrome—the runes that must
be deciphered and the moon-letters, whose very
existence is a secret.

The puns of *The Hobbit* are, by and large,
terrible, being of the excessively broad kind meant
to elicit groans—for example, the story of Bulroarer
Took who "charged the ranks of the goblins of
Mount Gram in the Battle of the Green Fields, and
knocked their king Golfimbul's head clean off with a
wooden club. It sailed a hundred yards through the
air and went down a rabbit-hole, and in this way the
battle was won and the game of Golf invented at the
same moment."

Though puns are sprinkled throughout, the riddles are concentrated in the Gollum and Smaug
episodes. As is appropriate, given the increasing stature of Bilbo and his adversaries, the riddles in the
Gollum episode are more "potted,"—"Chestnuts,
Chestnuts," as Gollum says. They do, however,
reflect the character of the two riddlers, as Gollum
consistently evokes natural forces in their deep, dark,
unhumanized aspect, while Bilbo evokes them in
their elevated, light, and social aspect. And while they
both tend toward the imagery of eating, Bilbo's use of
this imagery associates eating with nourishment,
while Gollum's associates it with destruction.

Having learned in a comic context the structure
of a riddling contest, made the more comprehensible
by the use of familiar riddles, the reader is prepared
for the original riddling Bilbo uses with Smaug. The
reader is also prepared for the notion that the outcome of the riddling can have consequences of
appalling severity—death and destruction, to be
precise.

Aside from the subject matter they carry, puns
and riddles add to the texture of the book because of
their qualities as language. Although one of the

truisms of children's literature is that moral ambiguity is inappropriate for the child reader, that
child is perfectly capable of dealing with some types
of linguistic ambiguity—and puns and riddles are
two of the types children have always loved. The
function of a pun or a riddle is to make the hearer or
the reader process the language on two levels simultaneously. One does not, then, as in reading ordinary,
straightforward prose, simply sample until one finds
the best meaning and then reject the other possibilities and go on. Rather, the reader does a double
take, seeing that both (or several) meanings are appropriate. Thus, for an instant, the reader pauses
over the language, enjoying it for itself as well as for
the story it advances.

A riddle functions in much the same way.
Mechanically, it is a pun in reverse, for one does not
stumble upon a riddle. Instead of meeting a word
that can be taken more than one way, given the context, the riddle reader meets an ambiguous description and tries to synthesize it in the answer. So the
successful response to a riddle is an achievement
more like making a pun than reading one. It is an
active enjoyment of the ambiguity of language rather
than a passive comprehension of it.

When Tolkien makes his puns and asks his riddles in *The Hobbit,* he is not only having his joke and
making allusions to conventions of Anglo-Saxon and
Middle-English literature, he is also involving the
reader in the very way that the language itself works
and provides an enjoyment of its own. He is helping
his readers to read as a philologist does.

Proverbs, though they are also traditionally a
kind of wordplay enjoyed by children, have an additional function in *The Hobbit.* In any culture, a familiar proverb such as "A stitch in time saves nine," or "A
rolling stone gathers no moss" is a pithy summary of

the point to be learned from a short tale dealing with a familiar situation. As such, it implies a social or cultural past with ages of experience that have been distilled to their essence. The proverbs of *The Hobbit* contribute to the sense of reality of the world within the story by giving us a sense that our story is just one episode in a history that may well be as long as our own. So Bilbo's " 'While there's life there's hope!' as my father used to say" and "Third time pays for all," echoing proverbs of our own primary world, make Tolkien's secondary world seem the more real for the similarity. At the same time, Bilboesque proverbs like "Every worm has his weak spot" and "Never laugh at live dragons" use the familiar proverb form to make the unfamiliar inhabitants of the secondary world seem more matter-of-fact. Again, we are seeing wordplay, but it is wordplay with a literary intent that extends beyond simple fun.

Although it is also fun, the use of runes, moon-letters, hand-drawn maps, and the other kinds of "cunning handwriting" Gandalf loves helps to create a sense of the past in *The Hobbit*. In addition, however, they are connected to the physical attraction of language, and especially that of secret language. There is a charm in the shapes of exotic letters and words that goes beyond any consideration of meaning into the realm of the purely aesthetic. But the runes and the moon-letters merge the physical attraction with the attraction of understanding meaning. Though Bilbo and the dwarves can respond to the runes on Thorin's map only as aesthetic objects, Gandalf, whose knowledge is greater, can understand their meaning as well, in the way that a student of another language could read it. But Elrond, who knows all about runes of every kind, illustrates the third and most important kind of understanding—that which requires a knowledge not only of the language but of the cultural context. The point of his finding and reading the moon runes is to allow Bilbo and the dwarves to find their way into the mountain. Without a clear understanding of the language, which is what Elrond provides, it is impossible to stand where the writer stood, to see what he saw. "Philology," said Tolkien in his Oxford Valedictory, "presented to lovers of poetry and history fragments of a noble past that without it would have remained forever dead and dark."[4] And that is what Elrond's mastery of language accomplishes in *The Hobbit*.

In addition to introducing his reader to the enjoyable qualities of language, Tolkien also explores or exploits in *The Hobbit* one of the popular theories of his time that dealt with the origin of the language, particularly as it concerned the role of naming in the evolution of language.

The theory that comes in for ridicule in *The Hobbit* is called the "Ding-dong theory." Promulgated by the German linguist, Max Müller, the "Ding-dong theory" of the origin of language argued that language was a "natural" phenomenon, like rocks or stars or donkeys, and that it could thus best be studied as a natural rather than as a historical event. More important, Müller argued that everything in nature had a "true" name, and that there was some mystic correlation between name and meaning. His metaphorical explanation of the way names were assigned to objects ran something like this: Every object in nature, when struck by another object, gives off its own particular sound. Similarly, when the mind of man is struck by the perception of a particular object, it gives off a unique sound. For example, the impact of the perception of a dragon on the human mind immediately gives rise to the sound, "Dragon."

Müller's argument was susceptible to ridicule by Tolkien not only because he himself repudiated it relatively soon, but also because it insisted on viewing a language as an independently existing natural object rather than as an historical artifact, the product of a particular culture. In the later years of the nineteenth century, Müller's theory was debunked. More important, Tolkien's own studies, which had convinced him that a language could not develop without a mythology, must have made Müller's theory seem both wrongheaded and pernicious. For Tolkien, a language was a historical object, beyond any doubt.

So when Gandalf announces himself to Bilbo with "I am Gandalf, and Gandalf means me," he is not simply introducing himself in the grand comic manner, though he certainly does that. Rather, he is making a statement about reality and the symbol (name) that represents it. "I am Gandalf" asserts the primacy of the real existence of a being, and "Gandalf means me" asserts the relationship between the speaker and the word that symbolizes him. The speaker exists whatever he is called, but the symbol *Gandalf* is appropriately used only to signify him. On the face of it, then, the object seems far more powerful than the symbol. But look at the differences in the responses the two elicit. For "the object" Bilbo has only a polite "good morning," but for the symbol he has a dramatic, poetic, imaginative response mixing memory and a longing for adventure that he may even have kept a secret from himself. It is really a very neat illustration of the power of the symbol:

Gandalf, Gandalf! Good gracious me! Not the wandering wizard that gave Old Took a pair of magic diamond studs that fastened themselves and never came undone till ordered? Not the fellow who used to tell such wonderful tales at parties, about dragons and goblins and giants and the rescue of princesses and the unexpected luck of widow's sons? Not the man that used to make such particularly excellent fireworks! . . . Bless me, life used to be quite inter—I mean, you used to upset things badly in these parts once upon a time.

The arbitrary quality of the relationship between object and name, and yet the necessity of having these arbitrary relationships if a reader is to find his way around in a fantasy world at all, is suggested by Gandalf's answer to Bilbo's question, "Why is [the great rock] called the Carrock?" "He [Beorn] called it the Carrock, because carrock is his word for it. He calls things like that carrocks, and this one is *the* Carrock because it is the only one near his home and he knows it well." The place-name, then, exists without really meaning much itself, but it provides Beorn with a part of a map of his world, and it provides the reader with one as well.

The arbitrary quality of names as a phenomenon of language is further illustrated by the treatment of the swords Gandalf and Thorin find in the trolls' cavern. The runes on the elvish blades reveal that, in the language of Gondolin, a lost city of the elves, the swords were named *Orcrist* (goblin-cleaver) and *Glamdring* (the foe-hammer). But in the language of the goblins, the same swords have utterly different names—*Biter* and *Beater*. As with Gandalf, the object remains the same whatever it is called, but the symbols for it carry meaning far beyond that implicit in the object itself. And for each group, it is as if the swords "are" what they are named in that language and are only "called" what they are named in the other.

At the same time as he appears to consider the scientific theories of the origin of language, Tolkien also hearkens back to the "Golden Age theory." This theory holds that in the golden days of the world's youth, everything was alive in the same way that people are alive. Rocks and trees, birds and woodland

animals, all could speak and could understand one
another. Nature was alive in a human way, and par-
ticipated in human affairs in a manner that is now
found only in fantasies and fairy tales. Thus Beorn,
who may be an original man "descended from the
first men," can communicate with all the animals.
Beorn's status as a skin-changer, a man who can,
when he wishes, assume the form of a bear, unites
him with nature in a way that makes his ability to
understand the language of animals seem to be simply a matter of common sense. His merging with
nature is, then, a physical parallel to the spiritual
union of the elves with nature expressed in the
Elvenking's understanding of the language of all nature as the news of Smaug's death spreads:

The Elvenking had received news from his own messengers and from the birds that loved his folk, and already
knew much of what had happened. Very great indeed was
the commotion among all things with wings that dwelt on
the borders of the desolation of the Dragon. The air was
filled with circling flocks, and their swift-flying messengers
flew here and there across the sky. Above the borders of the
Forest there was whistling, crying, and piping. Far over
Mirkwood tidings spread: "Smaug is dead!" Leaves rustled
and startled ears were lifted.

Part and parcel of this golden-ageism of Beorn and
the elves is the ability of Bard, the heir of the Lord of
Dale, who marvels to find that as the last of an ancient
race, he can understand the language of the thrush,
as the men of Dale did long ago. Thus linguistic
theories about the origin of language are seemingly
reduced to tautology and subjected to ridicule while
the mythic, or golden age, theory is developed with
sympathy.

The last major concern in the development of
the language theme is related to the power of the
symbol discussed earlier in the "I am Gandalf" pas-

sage. Throughout *The Hobbit* Tolkien extols the power of language, particularly literary language. From the first pages when the dwarves' song, "Far over the misty mountains cold," awakens "something Tookish" in Bilbo and makes him long for adventure, the power of language to entrance (as with the songs of the elves), to reveal the speaker's character (as with the language of the trolls and the Wargs), and to manipulate (as with Smaug and the Master of Esgaroth) is consistently expanded. It culminates in the image of Bard, descendant of the Lord of Dale, who is the godlike high-mimetic hero *par excellence*. That one whose name means *poet* should be a dragon-slayer and savior of his people, as well as a noble leader who seeks for both justice and mercy, is an unmistakable evocation of the power of language.

Though it would not, perhaps, be appropriate to say of *The Hobbit*, as Tolkien said of *The Lord of the Rings*, that it was "primarily linguistic in inspiration, it nevertheless seems clear that language is an important theme in *The Hobbit*. The light-hearted wordplay and the satiric treatment of some linguistic theories is appropriate to the comic tone of this first of Tolkien's fantasies, and though one could not say that the language theme is as important here as it is in later works, one cannot ignore its presence or deny that the language theme is another particular in which *The Hobbit* looks forward to *The Lord of the Rings*, and *The Silmarillion*.

3

The Quest as Legend:
The Lord of the Rings

When *The Hobbit* was so well received by the children's market, Allen and Unwin immediately approached Tolkien with the suggestion that he write a sequel—"More about Hobbits." Though Tolkien had continued to write about Middle-earth, and though he did want to publish more of his fantasies with Allen and Unwin, he did not have any more hobbit stories, but he agreed to try. As he began to write the story of Bilbo's nephew, one of the "nephews and nieces on the Took side" mentioned at the end of *The Hobbit,* Tolkien found himself becoming more and more interested in other characters—the elves and Elf-friends, wizards, those "masters of lore and good magic" who with Gandalf had succeeded in driving "the Necromancer from his dark hold in the south of Mirkwood," and, of course, the Ring.

Thus, although Tolkien began to write his sequel to *The Hobbit* in 1936, and although his publishers hoped it would be another children's book, *The Lord of the Rings,* Tolkien's second full-length work of fantasy, did not appear until 1954–55, and then its proper audience was not immediately apparent. It is an epic fantasy in three volumes, each volume containing two books, which traces the adventures of Bilbo's nephew, Frodo, and his friends as they struggle to beat back and destroy the evil Sauron and to restore peace to Middle-earth.

The Lord of the Rings is, without doubt, the most impressive and most successful of Tolkien's full-length works. Although it is long, it does not sprawl; rather the plot advances steadily and the subplots are integrated into the main plot neatly. The number of characters is large, but each one has a vivid and memorable existence for the reader. Most important, although the theme of *The Lord of the Rings,* like that of *The Hobbit,* is the unending struggle of good and evil, in the later work Tolkien has managed to make that basic dialectical struggle complex and interesting by daring to entertain the idea that a range of goods as well as a range of evils is possible in the world.

Volume one of the trilogy is *The Fellowship of the Ring.* In it, Bilbo's ring is revealed to be the "One Ring" of the ominous verse, "One Ring to rule them all, One Ring to find them, / One Ring to bring them all and in the darkness bind them." At Gandalf's urging, Frodo, his two friends, Pippin and Merry, and his gardener, Sam Gamgee, undertake to deliver the ring to Elrond, the Master of Rivendell. The journey is filled with dangers, including attacks from strange, formless, black-cloaked riders, one of whom wounds Frodo with a Morgul *(black-arts)* knife.

At Rivendell, Frodo is healed and the company discovers that uprisings of evil have sent representatives of all the "Free Peoples of the World" to Rivendell for counsel. When it is decided that the Ring must be destroyed and that Frodo must carry it to Mount Doom and throw it in the volcanic fires, the Fellowship of the Ring forms to accompany him. It comprises the four hobbits, Frodo, Sam, Pippin, and Merry; two men, Aragorn (the rightful king) and Boromir (the son of the Steward of Gondor); an elf,

Legolas, son of the King of Mirkwood; a dwarf, Gimli, son of Gloin; and the wizard, Gandalf.

Beset by forces of evil in the forms of nature, monsters, and Orcs, the fellowship experiences the deaths of Gandalf and Boromir before Frodo and Sam strike off on their own; Pippin and Merry are captured by Orcs; Aragorn, Legolas, and Gimli set off to rescue them.

Volume two, *The Two Towers,* tells of the reunion of Pippin and Merry with Aragorn, Gimli, and Legolas; the return of Gandalf (now called "The White"); and the alliance of the fellowship with the men of Rohan just as the forces of evil begin the siege of Gondor, seat of Aragorn's kingdom. Meanwhile, Frodo and Sam, found in the wastes by the creature from whom Bilbo took the Ring in *The Hobbit,* force Gollum to guide them to Cirith Ungol, the spider's pass, a less heavily guarded entrance to Mordor. Frodo is wounded by the giant spider, Shelob, and is captured by the Orcs.

Volume three, *The Return of the King,* recounts the heroic actions of men, elves, dwarves, and hobbits at the seige of Gondor, the acceptance of Aragorn as King of Gondor, and the assault of his armies on Mordor. Paralleling the military epic is the lonely trek of Frodo and Sam to Mount Doom, where Gollum suddenly reappears, snatches the Ring, and falls with it into the volcano. The heroes are reunited, evil is cast out of the kingdom, including the Shire where it has lately flourished, and the last of the fair folk, the elves, leave Middle-earth, taking Frodo and Bilbo, the Ring-bearers, with them. The reign of men begins.

The first difference one notes in moving from *The Hobbit* to *The Lord of the Rings* is the tone. The trilogy is not uniform in tone (Tolkien himself observed that the tone of Book One was very different from the rest), but it immediately sounds far more serious than *The Hobbit,* and the level of diction and the level of seriousness increase steadily as the locus of the story moves away from the Shire and its domesticity toward the stateliness of Rohan and the glory of Gondor. To understand how the tone of each work is appropriate is to begin to understand some of the essential differences between the two.

Structurally, as Randel Helms points out, *The Lord of the Rings* is *The Hobbit* writ large in that both works participate in the vision of the whole life of man as a quest.[1] That quest, however, is marked for all men by two great events: the coming of adulthood, with all the rights and privileges pertaining to it, and the coming of death. To borrow the paradigm developed by Joseph Campbell, author of *The Hero with the Thousand Faces,* there is one heroic life, and quest stories differ only as to how they make use of different parts of it.[2] *The Hobbit* clearly makes use of only the first half of the cycle, ending with the hero's passage into maturity. As a story of the beginning of a full and fulfilling adult life, the specifics of which we are left to imagine for ourselves, and as the tale of a young hobbit with his life before him, it is appropriately sunny, even comical, in tone. *The Lord of the Rings,* however, takes the hero completely through the cycle to the point of his essentially sacrificial death. Its somber tone is appropriate to the story of inevitable decline and death. In fact, the only time *The Lord of the Rings* sounds at all like *The Hobbit* is when Pippin and Merry, in the early chapters, indulge in some youthful foolishness. Even Sam, who is often seen as a vehicle for comic relief, is identified as serious from the early stages of Book One by his reverence for elves.

As the nature of transitional event toward which the plot moves differs in seriousness, so does the

social status of the characters. Bilbo is an ordinary
hobbit, comfortable, but surely not aristocratic—not,
in fact, extraordinary in any way. It is the function of
his story to show how the most ordinary young hobbit
may "have more to him than anyone suspects." The
dwarves with whom he travels are also identified as
ordinary folk. The party travels in weatherstained
cloaks, regards the adventure as a commercial enterprise, and, unable to find or afford a hero, settles for
a burglar instead.

   The Lord of the Rings, however, selects its personae
from the higher social orders. By virtue of Bilbo's
fortune and his status as Elf-friend, Frodo's social
and moral position is higher than Bilbo's was at the
opening of *The Hobbit.* The backgrounds of Pippin
and Merry are traced in the Prologue in such a way as
to establish their status as descendants of some of the
first families of the Shire.

   Similarly, while the elves of *The Hobbit* are silly,
capricious, and given to singing nonsense rhymes,
such as "tra-la-la-lally, come back to the valley," the
elves of *The Lord of the Rings* are glorious, responsible,
and poetic. Much has been made of Tolkien's evolv-
ing ideas of the nature of elves, and by the time the
first group of elvish travelers appears in *The Lord of
the Rings,* driving off the black riders with their hymn
to Elbereth, it is clear that we are dealing with a race
in whom the attributes of divinity are legion. The
appearance of the Elf-Lord, Glorfindel, whom Frodo
sees for a moment at the ford "as he appears on the
other side," Elrond's status as acknowledged leader
of all the free people of Middle-earth, and Galadriel's
mystical insights in Lothlórien all succeed in mirror-
ing the seriousness of the tone in the depiction of the
elves.

   The third race of heroes, men, also is represented by higher social orders in *The Lord of the*

Rings than in *The Hobbit*. While it is perhaps true that Bard foreshadows the character of Aragorn, his part in *The Hobbit* is small. *The Lord of the Rings*, on the other hand, gives over half of its space to the affairs of men, the quest of Aragorn and the matter of Gondor, in which the descent of men from the nearly mythic men of Númenor is central.

As Tolkien widened his focus in *The Lord of the Rings* to include the affairs of kings of men as well as hobbits, he simultaneously changed the nature of the quest in another way. *The Hobbit*, with its steady focus on Bilbo and his development, is a singularly good example of a quest story that is primarily concerned with personal or individual issues. Though some mention is made of issues that involve whole societies, especially in the recognition of one's duty to mankind, and the vision of the responsibilities of a leader to his people, the central thematic and structural concern is Bilbo's growth and development, and through him, individual human growth and development. *The Lord of the Rings*, however, though it is still concerned with the individual struggle as depicted in Frodo, as much more a social work, reflecting ideas about broad issues of social roles and responsibilities and cultural attributes. This social vision is one reason languages become so important in the latter work—languages both reflect and create cultures; and the life of a culture depends on its language: "Each language," wrote Waclaw Lednicki, "represents centuries of tragic efforts on the part of human beings to find an adequate expression for their feelings and thoughts about the universe. Indeed, every great language is a unique mirror of the landscape, of the air, of the sky—of all the natural surroundings in which it has developed."[3]

When we have observed that *The Lord of the Rings* differs from *The Hobbit* in being more serious in tone, in representing a higher social order, and in addressing social rather than personal issues, we have described a set of differences that contains three of the important distinctions between fairy tales and myths. The two forms have much in common, to be sure—the vision of life as a quest; the basic dialectical structure that sets a world of happiness, security, and peace against a world of humiliation, loneliness, and pain; and a cyclical pattern that depicts a movement from the bright world into the dark one and back again.[4] However, myth is typically more majestic, more spiritual, more concerned with life as it *ought* to be lived rather than as it *could* be. Bruno Bettelheim has observed that "A myth, like a fairy tale, may express an inner conflict in symbolic form and suggest how it may be solved—but this is not necessarily the myth's central concern. . . . [In myths] the divine is present and is experienced in the form of superhuman heroes who make constant demands on mere mortals. Much as we, the mortals, may strive to be like these heroes, we will remain always and obviously inferior to them."[5]

In *The Lord of the Rings,* then, we have a story that bridges the gap between fairy tale and myth. Though both elves and wizards and superhuman heroes are present, they are not quite central; instead, the story focuses on the fortunes of men and hobbits. Yet, the tone, the importance of social issues, and the hierarchical social structure marks the work as one which aspires toward the status of myth. This medial position of the trilogy is reflected in Tolkien's treatment of his three great themes: the hero, the nature of good and evil, and the function of language.

In calling *The Hobbit* a fairy tale, one says something about the quality of the heroism in it—that the hero, Bilbo, is a low-mimetic hero—one not significantly better than we in kind or degree. But in

The Lord of the Rings, we seem also to be reading the kind of story that deals with the doings of gods and godlike men. This shift in focus from the ordinary to the extraordinary does not result so much from a change in the conception of hobbits, who are still the beings most like us, as it does from Tolkien's decision to create a structure that brings men into the center of the action. When we speak of the men of *The Lord of the Rings,* we speak, without a doubt, of godlike men, those high-mimetic heroes who are beyond us in both kind and degree. The emergence of these heroes in Tolkien's second work mirrors his growing preoccupation with his own myth of a golden age. Yet *The Lord of the Rings* is not itself a golden age story; it is the story of a lull in the decline of a world that already looks back to a golden age and mourns its lost grandeur and nobility. Aragorn, for example, is the last of the Kings of the Númenórean line, that is, the last of men directly descended from the three houses of men that came into the world when the elves still lived in Middle-earth, and the last in whom the high blood has not mingled with that of other, lesser races.

But even in Aragorn, the noblest of men, Tolkien traces some falling off since the golden days. The kings of Númenor were, we learn, descended from Eärendil the Mariner, who, having chosen to cast his lot with the elves (the first-born) is immortal. His son Elros, first King of Númenor, having chosen to stay with men, was granted "a great life-span . . . many times that of men." But as his descendants grew suspicious of the Eldar and began to persecute those who wished to remain Elf-friends, and as their fear of death grew, their life-spans shortened. So the death of Aragorn comes when he has lived only "a span thrice that of the Men of Middle-earth."

The Steward of Gondor, Denethor, and his son Boromir, illustrate another degree of falling away, the result of mixing with men of lesser blood. What remains longest among the men of Gondor from their Númenórean heritage is their physical being—men of high blood are always "tall men and proud with sea-gray eyes." But in only a few do the spiritual attributes of the original men live on as they live in Aragorn. Thus Pippin's shock of recognition when he first sees Faramir: "Here was one with an air of high nobility such as Aragorn at times revealed, less high perhaps, yet also less incalculable and remote: one of the Kings of Men born into a later time, but touched with the wisdom and sadness of the Elder Race."

The differences between Boromir and Faramir is an expression of the difference in what they have inherited from their Númenórean past. Boromir has inherited the bearing and the appearance—the physical attributes—only. But Faramir has also the lore and wisdom of his past for he has studied the "ancient tales," and he loves his city "for her memory, her ancientry, her beauty, and her present wisdom." It is not only knowledge of the past but reverence for it and understanding of it that set Faramir apart, and that knowledge, reverence, and understanding are his links to the golden age.

The men of Middle-earth, then, though they are not as godlike as they once were (Faramir says, "We are become Middle Men, of the Twilight, but with memory of other things"), are by virtue of their inheritance, symbols of an order of mankind above us. The reader's perspective is more nearly that of Merry, who agrees that hobbits "can't live long on the heights" but adds, ". . . at least, Pippin, we can now see them, and honour them."

Thus, though they are high-mimetic heroes, the men of Middle-earth, as they are depicted in *The Lord of the Rings,* are not divine. Indeed, as Aragorn's

death (described in the Appendix) and the deaths of
Denethor and Théoden show, the inevitability of
man's death is one of the most important facts of his
existence. The heroic men of the trilogy occupy a
medial position between the everyman hero, the
Bilbo of *The Hobbit,* and the divine heroes of the
golden age.

In the heroes of men in *The Lord of the Rings,* we
can see a whole hierarchy of heroic possibilities. In
the men of Rohan, we see man as a purely physical
hero, the warrior who was in such short supply in *The
Hobbit.* The Rohirrim are "fair to look upon," and
"love war and valour as things good in themselves,
both a sport and an end." The power of the idea of
the warrior hero is so great that, though it is an
unpopular notion in our own time, it actually moved
Tolkien to unite the image of warfare with that of
creativity: In the battle of Pelennor fields, the men of
Rohan "burst into song, and they sang as they slew,
for the joy of battle was on them, and the sound of
their singing that was fair and terrible came even to
the city."

The men of Gondor, also brave, strong, and
physically adept, add to the image of the warrior hero
a spiritual quality that moves them up the heroic
ladder. The difference is the admiration the men of
Gondor have for "more skills and knowledge than
only the craft of weapons and slaying" which, if we
look to Faramir as an example, means being "a lover
of lore and of music" and a seeker after wisdom. By
exemplifying a hero who values the spiritual life of a
culture as well as its physical life, Faramir links the
Rohirrim to Aragorn, King of the Númenóreans.

Aragorn, with his transcendent beauty revealed
at moments such as the Council at Rivendell, the visit
to Cerin Amroth in Lothlórien, or the coronation in
Gondor, and his spiritual strength revealed by his

ability to turn the palantir away from Sauron and by his command of the oath-breakers, tops the hierarchy of heroes of men. Not only does he protect, as the Rohirrim, and preserve, as the stewards of Gondor, he also *creates* (literally, re-creates), bringing both physical and spiritual life to the people and to the land.

His first appearance as a healer occurs even before he is revealed as the king in exile, when he ministers to the wounded Frodo, victim of a black rider and his "morgul-knife." He treats the wound by bathing it with a water in which he has steeped *athelas,* "a healing plant that the Men of the West brought to Middle-earth." With the same *athelas* he treats the less serious wounds of Sam and Frodo after the escape from Moria and the death of Gandalf.

It is not until Aragorn enters the city of Gondor, in the echo of the old saying, "The hands of the King are the hands of a healer," that the common name of athelas is revealed—"kingsfoil . . . the country folk call it in these latter days." And the rhyme of the old wives foretells its virtues:

> When the black breath blows
> and death's shadow grows
> and all lights pass,
> come athelas! come athelas!
> Life to the dying
> In the king's hand lying!

As the wounded heroes in the Houses of Healing are called back to life by the baptismal bathing with *athelas,* so the land and the city are brought back to life with trees and fountains, likewise suggesting a renewal of fertility.

As king, Aragorn unites all the heroic qualities to become the most heroic of men: "Ancient of days he seemed and yet in the flower of manhood; and wisdom sat upon his brow, and strength and healing were in his hands." However, his own position as intermediary is made clear by his consistent consciousness that he must be instructed by others, such as Elrond and Gandalf, who, more than he, seemed attuned to the voices of beings beyond the world, whose existence seems to be wholly spiritual. Though the heroes of men approach the divine, they are human, not superhuman, and they see, as we do, that yet another level of heroism and another level of heroes must have preceded them.

Among the hobbits, Frodo is no more a traditional hero than Bilbo was before him. He is neither stronger than most men, nor braver than most. He is reluctant to take risks and is terrified by the implications of the Ring. Nor is he finally strong enough to resist its power.

But the heroic qualities Frodo does possess, though of less dramatic proportions than those of high-mimetic heroes, are sufficient to the task given him. Despite his fear, he has an unwavering commitment to the quest once he has undertaken it. He is selfless in his love for his companions. He is able to feel pity for even the tormented Gollum and the fallen Saruman, and he is willing to accomplish by sacrifice what he cannot hope to accomplish by strength. Most important, he is capable of carrying on when there is no hope.

Frodo's commitment to the quest is unquestionable. His understanding of the necessity for the quest begins with his conviction that what is good must be preserved and protected, an idea to which Tolkien returns, again and again: in Frodo's willingness to sacrifice himself for the Shire; in Bilbo's commitment to his "Translations from the Elvish"; in Faramir's desire to study the archives of Gondor under the tutelage of Gandalf; in the histories compiled by Pippin and Merry; and in the Red Book of Westmarch, kept by Sam and handed down through Elanor. A reverence for the past and its values is among the first of Frodo's virtues and an important motive for his quest.

Second among his heroic attributes is the willingness to sacrifice himself to preserve those things he values. His agreement to carry the ring into Mordor and probable destruction is a triumph of the will to serve over the will to live. During the council at Rivendell, Frodo is conscious only of his fear of the Ring and of the evil it represents. He is nearly as surprised as anyone else when he hears himself say, "I will take the ring . . . though I do not know the way."

In fact, despite the continual subconscious longings to give in to the power of the Ring, symbolized by his hand's continual straying toward it, Frodo never gives up his conscious decision to offer himself as a sacrifice until he stands at the crack of Doom. When at that moment the subconscious will to live and to assert power breaks through the conscious desire to sacrifice himself to destroy power, the result is symbolically the sacrificial death required, though the body sacrificed is that of Frodo's alter-ego, Gollum. Frodo has finished his spiritual quest by that time, however; he has completed his task and is ready to die, though Sam, who has much living to do yet, hopes on, saying, "I don't want to give up yet. It's not like me, somehow, if you understand."

From this point to the end, Frodo is essentially an inactive hero. Like Oedipus, in the course of saving his world he has become unable to be a part of it, so he remains only long enough to complete his share of the Red Book and thus to make possible the ritual re-creation of his sacrifice. As he tells Sam,

I tried to save the Shire, and it has been saved, but not for me. It must often be so, Sam, when things are in danger:

some one has to give them up, lose them, so that others may keep them. But you are my heir: . . . and you will read things out of the Red Book and keep alive the memory of the age that is gone, so that people will remember The Great Danger and so love their beloved land all the more.

But it is not only Frodo who is self-sacrificing and apotheosized. Of the other high-mimetic heroes, both Gandalf and Aragorn sacrifice much for the greater good. For Aragorn the sacrifice is appropriately one that only a ruler can make—to hold his own claims to happiness and well-being in abeyance until he can provide for his subjects. His sacrifice is therefore his long and lonely life as an outcast Ranger and his enduring love for Arwen Evenstar. Gandalf, like Frodo, is called upon for a sacrifice in a more circumscribed context. Like Frodo, Gandalf must offer his life, and like Frodo, he is willing to do so. Though the apotheosized Gandalf returns from his fall into the bottomless pits of Moria, his sacrificial offering of himself to save his friends from the Balrog is none the less heroic. Nor is Boromir's defense of Pippin and Merry from the Orcs less heroic because it fails, culminating in their capture and his death.

A third defining characteristic of the Tolkien hero is a courage that transcends mere physical bravery. From the first moment Frodo hears of the enemy and his connection with the Ring, he is afraid. At home in The Shire he is afraid and lonely and extremely conscious of the power of the enemy. At the parting of the paths that marks the breaking of the Fellowship, Frodo says to Boromir, "I know what I should do, but I am afraid of doing it, Boromir, afraid." And, of course, the effect of the Nazgûl is to strike fear into the hearts of men. But like Frodo, those men are heroes who feel the fear, acknowledge it, and then do what they must do despite it. In

Middle-earth, the shame is not in losing hope but in
letting despair immobilize one, as it does Théoden,
Lord of Rohan, or in letting it turn one to the service
of the dark, as Denethor, Steward of Gondor.

Instead of giving in or giving up to despair,
Tolkien's heroes must continually move forward.
Thus, though Aragorn moans that without Gandalf
the fellowship has no hope of succeeding in its mis-
sion, he also says, "We must do without hope." And
Sam, guarding the sleeping Frodo on the plains of
Gorgoroth, suddenly realizes that if they do reach
Mount Doom, they have no chance of returning:
"But even as hope died in Sam, or seemed to die, it
was turned to a new strength."

In *The Lord of the Rings,* then, Tolkien's heroes
are only in part traditional conquering heroes. They
are preeminently suffering heroes who persevere.
The status of the heroes as sufferers is psychologically, if not logically, connected to the next great
characteristic of the Tolkien hero—his mercy. On the
one hand, the heroes' mercy is part of the ethic that
"The hands of the King are the hands of healing,"
because the essence of mercy is the invitation to
reenter the good; that is, to reenter spiritual life or to
escape spiritual death. This must be the significance
of Gandalf's response to Frodo's judgment that Gollum deserves death: " 'Deserves it! I daresay he does.
Many that live deserve death. And some that die
deserve life. Can you give it to them? Then do not be
too eager to deal out death in judgement.' "

Mercy, in a Christian sense, refers specifically to
the heavenly reward that might be given to one who
has not earned it and cannot be expected to give
recompense for it. From the point of view of the
merciful, showing mercy means not paying one by
what he deserves, thus giving kind and compassion-
ate treatment to one who has no reason to expect it.

Here and in *The Hobbit,* the motive for mercy is pity, the hero's ability to feel and understand the pain and suffering implicit in the failure to be the best one can be. That is, pity is evoked by an awareness of the suffering of others, and in Middle-earth, suffering is inevitable. Physical pain, but also spiritual pain, is always possible and nearly always present, and no one is immune—not Gollum, who is ravaged by desire for the Ring; not Saruman, whose quest for power leads him to exile and thence to death; not Denethor, whose pride and love for his son leads him to death; not Frodo; not Gandalf; not Aragorn; not even Galadriel and Celeborn can escape suffering.

But to be able to pity others who suffer distinguishes the heroic from the villainous. In fact, Tolkien was no doubt making use of the philological fact that *pity,* in the general sense of "a feeling of compassion" did not exist as separate from its specific religious sense of *piety* until well after 1600: until then the ability to feel pity was a mark of piety.

Like Bilbo, who has been damaged so little by the Ring because he began his ownership of it with pity and mercy, Frodo finds reason to show compassion to Gollum. But unlike Bilbo, Frodo finds the motive for mercy in the commonality of his experience with Gollum's. Bilbo, we recall, was struck by the differences between the dark loneliness of Gollum's life and the sunny domesticity of his own. But by the time Frodo meets Gollum in *The Two Towers,* he too has felt the pain of loss and the burden of the Ring and is thus able to feel pity for the wretched creature.

Similar to Frodo's treatment of Gollum is Gandalf's treatment of the fallen Saruman when he offers Saruman the freedom to leave Orthanc, and Treebeard's release of Saruman after the defeat of Sauron. Aragorn's mercy is illustrated in his treatment of the army he leads to the Black Gate. When

the horror of the evil overcomes the army of the
King, Aragorn counsels,

"Go! . . . but keep what honour you may, and do not run!
And there is a task which you may attempt and not be
wholly shamed. . . ."
Then some being shamed by his mercy overcame their fear
and went on, and the others took new hope, hearing of a
manful deed within their measure that they could turn to,
and they departed.

There is an existential side to all of these instances of heroic mercy, for in *The Lord of the Rings*
mercy seems to mean the refusal to accept any being's
less than perfect state as his essential nature. Justice
would pay each according to what he has done; mercy
pays him according to what he might do—according
to the ideal. That is, those who are not a part of
Mordor are not evil because they were created to be
evil but because they have failed to live up to the level
of goodness inherent in them. In a sense, the act of
mercy works to preserve the free will of the receiver,
giving him the chance to become the better being that
is within his capability. Thus mercy is an essentially
creative act—it leaves the possibilities for a re-
creation of the self open as does any healing process.
As the hero shares with a divine being the quality of
mercy, he shares with him his creative power.

Finally, the heroes of *The Lord of the Rings* are
selfless in their love for their companions. This quality, like the others, is expressed differently in the
different characters, according to their mimetic level.
It is for love of the Shire and for love of mankind (the
Free Peoples) that Frodo undertakes the quest. But it
is his selflessness that leads him away from the company above the Falls of Raumos, for he is loath to
lead them further into danger. This selflessness is
matched, however, by Sam's unwavering determina-

tion not to let his master go on alone. Sam, as Frodo's servant and as a being with free will, exhibits a selflessness that yields perseverence unmatched by any of the abject slaves of Sauron, and in doing so illustrates the superiority of love freely given over force, no matter how strong.

This caring for the health, safety, and happiness of others is simply a less elevated version of the more godlike concern of Aragorn, in whom it is revealed that "The hands of the King are the hands of the healer."

As is true of the concept of heroism, the ideas of the nature of good and evil are markedly more complex in *The Lord of the Rings* than in *The Hobbit.* So great is the richness and extent of the trilogy that in it the moral issue is not simply good versus evil, but goods versus evils.[6] Tolkien's view of the universe here is that it is not simply dualistic but pluralistic, and there is room in a pluralistic world for a multitude of goods and evils.

On the positive side, the trilogy presents a range of goods, represented by the members of the fellowship. The range may be described as a hierarchy, although it is a hierarchy of kinds, not degrees, ranging from the earthly to the divine. Gandalf the Grey, later Gandalf the White is a representative of a good that suggests knowledge of the whole of experience and that actively opposes the evils it sees, from the most elemental (the Balrog, against which only Gandalf has any power) to the merely human (Wormtongue). His breadth of vision and his range of power suggest that his is a force for good that might well be called divine.

A more limited (because more human) range of good is represented by Aragorn, King of Gondor, whose power over the natural or elemental evils is indicated by his power of healing, and whose immersion in the more earthly aspects of heroic conduct, as when he rides into battle with the sword of Isildur gleaming before him, marks him as a hero of men. Where Gandalf's importance on the field of physical battle is primarily symbolic or psychological, Aragorn's is both symbolic and practical, as is appropriate for the last true son of the West and the betrothed of Arwen Evenstar, daughter of Elrond Half-elven.

As Aragorn's good is to Gandalf's, Boromir's is to Aragorn's. Boromir, a descendant of the Stewards of Gondor who have through the years become less like the Númenóreans and more like ordinary men, is in every way a physical hero. He is himself stunningly attractive—tall, strong, well-proportioned, and well-spoken. He is chiefly distinguished by his physical prowess—though he is ultimately overpowered, he kills legions of Orcs before succumbing. But his spiritual ties are more limited than those of Gandalf or of Aragorn. When he blows the horn of Gondor at need, only his brother and his father hear it. His fate does not have the cosmic implications of the fate of a Gandalf or an Aragorn.

Boromir's goodness is, then, limited to an active goodness. He is brave, he is adept, and he is a great warrior. But he is limited in his ability to understand the nature of the evil he must oppose. Like Gandalf and Aragorn, he has seen the evil of the Dark Lord face to face, but he has failed to understand it as anything more than a physical evil—a force that, in his view, simply must be met by greater force. His continued insistence that he would use the Ring for good, and should thus be given it serves only to illustrate his failure to understand that evil has its own existence and will not be transformed by anyone.

Though Boromir can be described as limited in goodness because, having seen, he only partially understands the nature of the evil that threatens his world; the hobbits are even more limited than he. The innocent folk of The Shire are, until the Black Riders appear, utterly unaware of the evils that stalk their borders. Yet in the course of the quest, Frodo comes to an understanding of the totality of the moral world, both the good side and the evil, that rivals Gandalf's perception. The equality of the perceptions of the two is perhaps most poignantly suggested in the image of the two of them riding, together with Bilbo and the elves, to the Grey Havens to sail into the sunset. But the hobbits who never leave the Shire also grow in their knowledge of good and evil when Sharkey and his men take over the Shire and transform it until Frodo can truly say, "Yes, this is Mordor." Tolkien suggests that the hobbits' ignorance of evil is part of their vulnerability to it.

As a pluralistic world has room for multiple goods, it also has room for multiple evils, ranging from the simple greed and envy of the Sackville-Bagginses to the conscious and unmitigated malice of Sauron. At intermediate points are betrayal by the quisling Bill Ferny of Bree, the warped hatred of Gollum, the inbred violence and perversions of the Orcs, and the elemental evil of Shelob and the Balrog. As the hierarchy of goods ranged from the human to the divine, the hierarchy of evils ranges from the human to the demonic. And the most demonic evil is Sauron.

Evil, as Tolkien conceives of it in *The Lord of the Rings,* is not unique in its forms or attributes: Like other evils in the western tradition, Sauron is *dark*—he is variously the Dark Lord, the Dark Power, or the Power of Darkness. His ancient home is the Dark Tower of Mordor, the Land of Shadows, and his messengers are the Dark Riders. The very uttering of his language is enough to cause a shadow to pass over the sun, and the years of his domination are called the Black years.

As it is reflected in Sauron, evil is closely allied with a quest for power. Here the notion of power goes beyond the simple acquisitiveness of *The Hobbit* to include the ultimate control—control over being. Sauron's power, or the power he seeks, is a power that parodies the power of the creator. Rather than create, Sauron will destroy; rather than set free, he will enslave; rather than heal, he will harm. The desire of Sauron to make everything in Middle-earth less than it is capable of being is clear in his repeated threats to "break" captives, in the ruined and desolate lands that were once fertile and productive, and in the Orcs and trolls, his parodies of men and dwarves (or as Treebeard would have it, of elves and ents).

Sauron's title, The Lord of the Rings, also suggests the enduring quality of evil, the quality that makes a final victory impossible. Though Sauron was "vanquished" when Isildur, the patriarch of Aragorn's line, cut the Ring from his finger, and though Sauron was caught in the wreck of Númenor and "the bodily form in which he long had walked perished," evil cannot be completely destroyed. It can be temporarily defeated; it can be set back; in the vision of *The Lord of the Rings*, it cannot be finally removed from the world.

In addition to being enduring, the evil of *The Lord of the Rings* is insidious. That is, the Ring as an extension of Sauron and thus as an embodiment of evil corrupts those who lust after it, those who accept it only from good motives, and those who take it knowing nothing of its nature, as the compulsion of Gollum, the fall of Boromir, the inability of Frodo to complete the quest, and the "stretching" of Bilbo all show.

Tolkien suggests, then, that every man contains the seeds of evil and that the seeds may be brought to germination by exposure to evil. Thus Gandalf, Aragorn, Faramir and Galadriel reject the Ring because though each of them has power of his own, they each know that even with the best intentions they could not control the Ring and change it from a power for evil to a power for good. That is, the Ring is not evil simply because it is powerful; it is inherently evil because it was born of evil, and it cannot therefore be made good, even by Gandalf or Galadriel.

The insidiousness of evil makes Tolkien's version of the sacrificing hero even more poignant and moving than its archetype. Frodo's danger is not simply a danger to his physical life, with the assurance of a reward in another world; he risks his spiritual life as well, for the very proximity to the Ring that will allow him to save the world threatens to make of him the source of its destruction. That is, on the edges of the cracks of doom the Ring succeeds in making of Frodo a hobbit Sauron. He claims the Ring, and it is taken from him as it was taken from Sauron at the end of the Second Age, by the severing of his finger.

This pairing of Frodo with Sauron not only suggests the dual nature of man, it also suggests just how close Frodo has come to becoming the enemy he has offered his life to defeat. The ultimate defeat, then, in *The Lord of the Rings* is not simply to lose the battle with evil, but to become incorporated into it.

That such a danger exists (and its presence is equally clear in the lives and fates of Denethor, Wormtongue, and Saruman, all once good men who fell away from the good and became the servants of Sauron) suggests that Tolkien is working with a notion of man as a creature "strong enough to stand, but free to fall."

In developing the idea that the Ring is inherently evil, and in exploring the notion that good men may *become* evil, Tolkien has moved beyond the idea that evil is a simple absence of good. Though the capabilities for good and evil coexist in some characters, evil has for Tolkien a real and independent existence. The eschatological view of *The Lord of the Rings* is thus not one which foresees the conversion of evil to good, but one which sees that evil must conquer or be conquered.

The conception of evil as a force that has being of its own raises in all mythologies the question of the origin of evil, and Tolkien's mythology is no exception on this point. Most of the reflections on the origin of evil in *The Lord of the Rings* occur in the Appendices to the trilogy where it appears that even during the First Age there was an enemy (Morgoth) who poisoned the two trees that gave light to the land of the Valar and who stole the Silmarilli, the jewels in which the light of the two trees was preserved. Hence, evil entered Middle-earth before the elves. It is, then, coeval with the world. Evil was able to act among the Eldar because of the familiar weaknesses of character—e.g., pride and willfulness.

After the defeat of Morgoth, his servant Sauron appeared to be the plague of men. As pride and self-will were the weaknesses of the Eldar, fear of death was the weakness that brought men low and brought to an end the Second Age. Evil is thus a hydra-headed monster that takes whatever form the time requires.

Although Frodo, Aragorn, Gandalf, and Sam are the heroes of *The Lord of the Rings,* there is a sense in which the trilogy is Sauron's—he is the Lord of the Rings, and as the embodiment of evil, he is the force that initiates and perpetuates the action. But his importance to the trilogy extends beyond simple matters of plot to include more complex matters of theme, for he provides the work with a central image of evil and with the beginnings of a theory of the origin of evil.

Sauron's evil is directly opposed to Aragorn's heroism—rather than healing men, he would "break" them. The Mouth of Sauron who meets the armies of Gondor at the Black Gate tells them that Frodo's fate shall be to "endure the slow torment of years, as long and slow as our arts in the Great Tower can contrive, and never [to] be released, unless maybe when he is changed and broken, so that he may come to you, and you shall see what you have done." The motif of breaking or deforming is consistently with Sauron. Théoden's counselor, Wormtongue, is a snake who was once a man, a queer twisted sort of creature, and by the time of the Scouring of the Shire, a being who crawls like a dog. Similarly, Gollum was once an inquisitive and curious being "of hobbit-kind," but under the influence of the Ring he became mean-spirited, wretched, as the Ring began to "[eat] up his mind." When Sauron does create, he can only counterfeit. Treebeard the Ent tells Pippin and Merry, "Trolls are only counterfeits, made by the Enemy in the Great Darkness, in mockery of Ents, as Orcs were of Elves."

Parallel to the destruction or breaking of the creatures of Middle-earth, the destruction of the earth itself is a dramatic manifestation of evil. To follow Saruman is to follow death, to be sure, but Tolkien's images of death are most powerful when they depict the destruction of the land, the source of life itself. Again, the cultivated fertility of The Shire with its flower gardens ("snapdragons and sunflowers, and nasturtiums trailing all over the turf walls and peeking in at the round windows"), its meadows and hedges, contrasts with the wild beauty

of Ithilien, "the garden of Gondor now desolate,"
which, as it "had only been for a few years under the
dominion of the Dark Lord . . . was not yet wholly
fallen into decay," but it contrasts even more vividly
with the lands that have been long under his sway.
The Brown Lands near the border are desolate, "long
formless slopes stretching up and away toward the
sky; brown and withered they looked, as if fire had
passed over them, leaving no living blade of green: an
unfriendly waste without even a broken tree or a bold
stone to relieve the emptiness."

Nearer Mordor, desolation becomes hell. North
of the Black Gate "[t]he gasping pools were choked
with ash and crawling mud, sickly white and grey, as
if the mountains had vomited the filth of their en-
trails upon the lands about." And inside Mordor the
plains of Gorgoroth, which Sam and Frodo cross on
the last leg of their journey to Mount Doom, are
equally hellish: ". . . what from a distance had seemed
wide and featureless flats were in fact all broken and
tumbled. Indeed the whole surface of the plains of
Gorgoroth was pocked with great holes, as if, while it
was still a waste of soft mud, it had been smitten with
a shower of bolts and huge slingstones. The largest
of these holes were rimmed with ridges of broken
rock, and broad fissures ran out from them in all
directions."

The contrast between fertile growth and sterile
destruction is further developed in the two images of
restoration that close the trilogy. Aragorn's ascent to
the top of Mount Mundolluin after he has been
crowned reveals "the towers of the City far below
them like white pencils touched by the sunlight, and
all the vale of Anduin was like a garden, and the
Mountains of Shadow were veiled in a golden mist."
Less elevated but equally important is the work of
restoration Sam accomplishes in the Shire after

Saruman has cut down trees, installed smoke-belching and pollution-producing machines, built rows of cheap and nasty houses, and generally tried, as one Shiredweller puts it, "to make the Shire into a desert." Like the good gardener he is, Sam replants the Shire and, we are told, "tried to restrain himself from going round constantly to see if anything was happening." When trees accomplish twenty years' growth in one, when the air is full of "richness and growth," and when all the children are born fair and strong, the Shire has plainly been restored.

If the nature of evil in Middle-earth is that it is eternal and that it is insidious and thus widely threatening, if the attractions of evil are such that neither men nor wizards, dwarves nor hobbits are immune, we may wonder what factors constitute the weaknesses of evil. Why, in short, does evil fail in Middle-earth?

As W. H. Auden pointed out, the greatest weakness of evil is a lack of imagination—". . . for, while Good can imagine what it would be like to be Evil, Evil cannot imagine what it would be like to be Good."[7] From Galadriel to Sam, those in the service of good can imagine what would become of them if they tried to use the Ring. Indeed, the portrait of Frodo being pulled further and further into the darkness as he begins to be unable to call on memories of the good provides the reader with imaginative access to Tolkien's idea of what it is to be evil. He begins to see what it would be like not to be able to imagine good. Sauron simply cannot imagine that anyone could resist using the Ring and so is unlikely to suspect that anyone would ever try to destroy it.

Everywhere we look in *The Lord of the Rings,* we see evidence of the lack of imagination of evil, most clearly in the inability of evil to perform the basic imaginative act: creation. It is said, for example, that

Orcs are either men broken to Sauron's will or beings created as parodies of dwarves or elves. It is further said that Orcs and trolls do not even have languages of their own, ". . . but took what they could of other tongues and perverted it to their own liking." Even the One Ring, which was made by Sauron, could be made only after he lured the elvensmiths of Eregion into his service and learned their secrets. And, paradoxically, the smithies and furnaces of Isengard, with their iron wheels revolving and their hammers thudding, like the poorly built houses and the mills that belch smoke and stench in the Shire, are more represented as symbols of destruction than of creation.

One may thus be tempted to set up or to postulate some dialectical split between the natural and the artificial that will parallel a split between goods and evils, but Tolkien's version of reality is not quite that simple. It is true that machines are identified with evil in *The Lord of the Rings,* from the smithies of Isengard to the horrible catapults with which the Orcs throw the severed heads of the slain into the citadel of Minas Tirith, to the battering rams that break down the gates of that city. However, it is also true that elves and dwarves are makers or artisans, making for Minas Tirith gates "wrought of mithril and steel" as well as mail, swords, and shields. So it is not simply that to make, construct, or fashion flies in the face of nature. What, then, makes the difference between the tainted efforts of Saruman and Sandyman and the admirable efforts of the elves and dwarves?

Certainly a central point of differentiation is the aesthetic sensibility—even the most functional items made by dwarves and elves, swords, say, or the rope that Sam carries across the wastes, are made beautifully. The helmets and shields of the men of Gondor

and Rohan are elaborately styled and decorated and
the elven cloaks, like the ropes, are "strong, silken to
the touch, [and] grey of hue." The arts and crafts of
the elves unite them with nature and celebrate the
implicit sacredness or magical quality of nature
through the workmanship. The cloaks the travelers
are given in Lórien are "grey with the hue of twilight
under the trees . . .; and yet if they were moved, or set
in another light, they were green as shadowed leaves,
or brown as fallow fields by night, dusk silver as water
under the stars." And the paddles of the elven boats
have "broad leaf-shaped blades." The secret of the
beauty, and hence the positive qualities of the arts of
the elves, is explained by the leader of the group that
gives the cloaks to the travelers: "Leaf and branch,
water and stone: they have the hue and beauty of all
these things under the twilight of Lórien that we love;
for we put the thought of all that we love into all that
we make."

Thus the differences between the mechanic arts
of the Free Peoples and those of the servants of the
Dark Lord are two: the Free Peoples create in evocation or celebration of nature, in a preindustrial attitude which sees the world as essentially integrated
(with people as part of nature), while the servants of
Sauron create in an industrial mode which intends to
distinguish among parts of the world by setting some
elements above others (Sauron above creatures,
machines above natural forces). Moreover, the Free
Peoples produce from love while Morgul production
arises from hatred.

The attitude reflected in the Morgul arts is one
that celebrates distortion in nature. The livery of
the Orcs of Barad-dûr, for example, is marked by a
red eye, and the guard of the Tower of Cirith Ungol
bear "a Moon disfigured with a ghastly face of
death." And in contrast with the heroes' dwarfish

mithril mail and elven cloaks, the Orcs wear "long hairy breeches of some unclean beast-fell, and a tunic of dirty leather."

Many writers on Tolkien have commented on the nostalgia of *The Lord of the Rings,* the sense of longing for an earlier time when man was closer to nature and society was less industrialized, when the unity of the world was more apparent.[8] It is perhaps not surprising that these qualities and this time are closely associated with the elves, and the elves, their attitudes, their values, and their ways are closely bound up with the idea of good in *The Lord of the Rings.*

In contrast to evil, good in *The Lord of the Rings* is preeminently natural. Elves are known as The People of the Forests as dwarves are known as The People of the Mountains. The Tower Guard of Osgiliath takes for its crest a pair of white wings, and the men of Rohan ride to the sign of the White Horse. Aragorn's banner combines earth and air in the device of seven stars and one white tree. Thus the symbols of the powers for good in the trilogy are contrasted with evil not only by the contrast of black with white, but also by the contrast of the natural (trees and stars) with the human (the Red Eye of Barad-dûr and the White Hand of Saruman).

Good is also connected with nature in the trilogy by its character as a creative, life-giving force. First among the instances of this must be the folk wisdom of Gondor, "The hands of the King are the hands of a healer." This proverb unites the ideas of goodness, heroism, and creativity in the single symbol, *athelas.*

The chief characteristic of the *athelas* is its fragrance, which is its atmosphere-changing property. To the wounded, the fragrant steam is refreshing and strengthening, driving out both physical and spiritual pain. To them, and those about them, it calls

up earlier, happier times and the strength that accompanies such memories. It clears and calms their
minds; it lightens their hearts, it smells like "a memory of dewy mornings of unshadowed sun in which
the fair world in Spring is itself but a fleeting memory," or it smells as if "a keen wind blew through the
window, and it bore no scent, but was an air wholly
fresh and clean and young, as if it had not before
been breathed by any living thing and came new-
made from snowy mountains high beneath a dome of
stars, or from shores of silver far away washed by seas
of foam," or "like the scent of orchards, and of
heather in the sunshine full of bees."

Jane Nitzsche in *Tolkien's Art* rightly observes
that the three responses to the *athelas* reflect the
renewal of the three human faculties, rational, ap-
petitive, and sensitive.[9] However, it is equally
significant that the three victims of the great battle
wake to impressions of those things that are most
important to them. For Faramir, the image of "some
land of which the fair world in Spring is but a fleeting
memory" is appropriate because it evokes the pervasive myth of the golden age, to which he has always
felt allegiance, though to his father's sorrow. For
Éowyn, the image of unbreathed air and high stars is
appropriate because it represents the purity for
which she has pined during the long years she has felt
her life and that of her race being defiled by the
works of Wormtongue. Placed next to the elevated
images associated with Éowyn, those associated with
Merry strike the reader as distinguished by their
domesticity. The evocation of orchards, heather, and
bees is an evocation of the rural paradise that is the
Shire.

What this tailoring of sense impressions to the
greatest joys of the three wounded warriors suggests
is that *athelas* heals by helping people to be more fully

themselves. To be well is to be individual, which is to be free. Thus, though Aragorn creates Faramir, Éowyn, and Merry (in the sense that he is responsible for their rebirths), he creates them to be free, to be themselves, not to be bound to him.

Though the idea of healing is prominent in Tolkien's conception of the good, it is also associated with other kinds of creative or life-giving behavior. A great deal of the creativity associated with the good is linguistic, including Bilbo's ballad of Eärendil, all the heroic myths of the Eldar, and, as Frodo and Sam remind us, the creation of the story of *The Lord of the Rings*. Such joy in the uses of language is also reflected in the delight in names and naming felt by the elves and men, as, for example, Aragorn, son of Arathorn, Isildur's heir, Elessar, the Elf-stone and the Renewer, Strider of the house of Telcontar. The practice of naming and renaming continually reaffirms the existence of the good and, in that sense, continually re-creates it. Tolkien contrasts this practice with the tendency not to name evil at all if it can be helped, particularly on the part of Faramir, for to name is to create.

Closely related to linguistic creativity is the question of the kinds of information sources that can be trusted. Though supernatural sources of information are available (the palantíri), like the Ring's power, the usefulness of their information varies according to the characteristics of the user. Thus Denethor's use of the palantír drives him to despair and Saruman's seduces him to evil, for even the stones of Westernesse may be turned to the service of evil.

What is worthy of trust, then, is the creative and the individual—the literature and lore of the ancient days and the intuition of the individual. From the literature and lore of the ancient days come history,

motivation, and prophecy, and though the stories
may be dismissed (as by Ted Sandyman) or misunderstood (as by the Master of the Houses of Healing),
they speak true to those who listen. From individual
intuition comes a sense of where the public and the
private dreams overlap and why, therefore, the
myths of the ancient days are important and true.

The trustworthiness of traditional and intuitive
knowledge is a part of the larger value of respect for
the past. Respect for the old tales and the refusal to
assign them merely to the nursery or to the "cracked"
is an attribute of both pragmatic and absolute good.
On the pragmatic level, the usefulness of the information gained from the traditional sources is clear.
From the old books Gandalf has learned the secret of
the Ring. From the advice of the ancient seer,
Aragorn is reminded to ride the Path of the Dead.

But it is not only, or even primarily, for such
immediately pragmatic purposes that reverence for
the past is valued. More significantly, and more generally, the literature and lore of the ancient days of
Middle-earth, like the literature and lore of our own
world, reflect the continuities of earthly human
existence. The point is not that the story of Beren and
Lúthien Tinúviel is recapitulated in the story of
Aragorn and Arwen Evenstar, but that, for example,
Beren's quest for the Silmaril, his love of Lúthien, his
suffering for her sake, and his heroic death invoke
not just the sorrows and joys, the triumphs and defeats of Aragorn, but of all the children of earth, as
Sam realizes: "Beren now, he never thought he was
going to get that Silmaril from the Iron Crown in
Thangorodrim, and yet he did, and that was a worse
place and a blacker danger than ours." For Sam as for
all of us, myths exist as myths because they say something to the human spirit, something that remains
worth saying even though the meaning, not just the

story, is ages old. And therein lies the connection between the theme of the nature of good and evil and the uses of language in *The Lord of the Rings.*

As Tolkien expanded his thinking about the nature of heroes and heroism from *The Hobbit* to *The Lord of the Rings,* and as he grew subtler in his thinking about good and evil, he also enlarged the role of language in his imaginative world. One can see in *The Lord of the Rings* the same kind of use of wordplay as Tolkien enjoyed in *The Hobbit,* though the riddles, puns, and proverbs are more serious in tone and more heroic in purpose. Tolkien goes beyond the mere linguistic fun of *The Hobbit* to reflect in his history of Middle-earth the interpenetrations of language and culture. He constructs languages for the people of his imaginative world and then investigates what those languages suggest about the cultures from which they come. The magnitude of his achievement is clear when we consider that in undertaking this task of philological investigation of an imaginative world, Tolkien hardly misses a beat in the progress of the narrative. One rarely feels that the professor has stepped out of his role as a fantasist to lecture, at least until one reaches the appendices.

In *The Hobbit* Tolkien used proverbs to increase the sense of reality with which the reader meets the imaginary world. In *The Lord of the Rings* he goes further, using proverbs to build the sense of the familiar, but also to create a sense of the individuality of cultures. The proverbs, as groups, refer to Anglo-Saxon and Middle English sources,[10] but they have the effect, even for readers who do not recognize the references, of lending a solidity to the projection of Middle-earth. A culture that has its own folk-wisdom, whether it is the same as ours or only parallel to it, is a culture that seems to make sense, to have coherence, to operate by rules of some kind—in short, to seem real.

In general, there are two possible uses for proverbs in literature: they may be intended to instruct or to entertain. It is unlikely that Tolkien's intent in *The Lord of the Rings* is to instruct, because he often amuses himself and the reader by creating situations in which obvious statements of traditional wisdom are set in opposition, as when Elrond reminds the nine walkers of their freedom to reject the quest at any time:

"Faithless is he that says farewell when the road darkens," said Gimli.
"Maybe," said Elrond, "but let him not vow to walk in the dark, who has not seen the nightfall."
"Yet sworn word may strengthen quaking heart," said Gimli.

Like the classic opposition, "He who hesitates is lost," and "Look before you leap," Gimli's exchange with Elrond suggests the limitations of the partial truths of proverbs as guides to action.

If Tolkien's purpose in using proverbs is not simply to instruct, then it is likely to be to entertain, and Tolkien's entertaining uses of proverbs are many and varied. He uses proverbs to cap climaxes or to emphasize situations, as when Aragorn's entry into the city of Gondor is met with "The hands of the King are the hands of a healer," or when Faramir reveals that he is Boromir's brother with "Night oft brings news to near kindred." He uses proverbs seriously, as when Aragorn applauds Pippin's using his brooch from Lórien as a trail marker during his capture by the Orcs, saying, "One who cannot cast away a treasure at need is in fetters." Or he uses them humorously, as when Gandalf says of Barliman Butterbur,

"He can see through a brick wall in time (as they say in Bree)." But most of all, he uses proverbs to heighten the sense of identity of a single character or group.

Barliman's string of platitudes, "It never rains but it pours, as we say in Bree" and ". . . there's no accounting for East and West, as we say in Bree" is perfect as a representation of the conversation of a man who is too busy to concentrate on what is before him. This sort of nearly meaningless utterance is only probable in a kind of semiconscious conversation that prepares us for a shock of recognition instead of a simple shock when Barliman reveals that he has forgotten to send Gandalf's warning letter to Frodo.

On the other hand, the serious, thoughtful, almost stately character of the men of Rohan is reflected in the phrasing of their proverbs: "Where will wants not, a way opens" or "Oft evil will shall evil mar." There is about these proverbs an archaic feeling, in part the result of word choice (*oft, froward*) and in part a function of Tolkien's having rendered a familiar thought in unfamiliar syntax, such as "Need brooks no delay, but late is better than never."

The reader's tendency to identify most closely with the hobbits is strengthened by the similarity of their traditional wisdom to our own. Sam's "Where there's life there's hope" and his "Handsome is as handsome does" are familiar in word, phrase, and meaning, whereas a proverb like Gandalf's "The burned hand teaches best," while familiar in sentiment, is probably better known in its "Once burned, twice shy" form.[11]

It would not be precisely true to say that there is less wordplay in *The Lord of the Rings* than in *The Hobbit*. It does seem to be true, however, that the proportion is smaller. Proverbs are still abundant and seem to be used toward a multitude of literary ends, including the development of character. Actual rid-

6 2 2 .13

dles are much less in evidence, though the sense of
the world as a riddle, or an enigma, is much more
pervasive here than in the earlier work. Similarly,
puns are much less apparent here, though it may be
only that they are subtler, as when Goldberry recognizes Frodo as an Elf-friend by "the ring in your
voice."

But of central interest to any discussion of language in *The Lord of the Rings* is the trouble Tolkien
takes to develop his technique of using differences in
language to differentiate among races, and, in many
cases, to suggest the character of the various races.
Each of the major groups of *The Lord of the Rings* has
its own language, and even the nonphilologist perceives how the language reflects the racial character
of its speakers. One should note, however, that the
language of the trilogy purports to be a translation in
all cases; thus the reader is driven to the extensive
appendices to find Tolkien, "the translator's," explanation of the nature of the original languages and the
decisions he found necessary for the translation.

Hobbits, for example, speak what is called the
Common Speech. Their vocabulary is generally simple and unexotic, as is their sentence structure, although the educated among them speak more formally, causing nearly all who meet them to comment
on their verbal charm, as when Beregond tells Pippin
". . . strange accents do not mar fair speech, and hobbits are a fair-spoken folk." Hobbits, it seems, are a
race of chatterers, who ". . . will sit on the edge of ruin
and discuss the pleasures of the table, or the small
doings of their fathers, grandfathers, and great-
grandfathers, and remoter cousins to the ninth
degree. . . ." For them, that is, language is fundamentally a social tool. They are great talkers, great
storytellers, and, at least among the more admirable,
great lovers of poems, songs, and stories. Bilbo's

translations from the Elvish and his Red Book may be anomalous, but Sam's love of stories of elves and his memory of the old nonsense rhyme about "oliphunts," as well as Frodo's tendency to be moved to poetic expression when he leaves home or when he meets Goldberry, suggest that as language users, hobbits have more to them than first meets the ear.

More indication of the hobbits' characteristic uses of language is to be found in the narrator's commentary on the habitual humming and singing of the hobbits. He observes that hobbits "have a way" of singing, ". . . especially when they are drawing near to home at night." And at the same time as he establishes the basically domestic and social nature of hobbit language use, he points out the unusual qualities of Frodo, Sam, and Pippin, who sing not of supper and bed, but of the joys of the open road.[12]

Hobbits consider conversation one of the chief joys of social life, as is demonstrated by Merry's desire to sit and talk herb lore with Théoden, King of Rohan; they also appreciate the social character of literary utterance, for the folk in the Prancing Pony enjoy a bit of a song as much as the folk of Elrond's haven of Rivendell, though the celebration of "brown beer" in Frodo's song about the man in the moon is much less elevated in subject matter and diction than Bilbo's ballad of Eärendil, which is, in turn, less elevated than the Elven hymn, "A Elbereth Gilthoniel." The elves of *The Lord of the Rings* speak one of two languages: Quenya (High-Elven) or Sindarin (Grey-Elven). By the time of *The Lord of the Rings*, Quenya is only a literary rather than a social language, and thus appears only in songs such as "A Elbereth Gilthoniel." But the elves of Rivendell and the elves of Lothlórian and Mirkwood, whether descended from the High Elves or the Grey Elves, speak a variety of Sindarin.

Whether Quenya or Sindarin or Common Speech, the language of the elves is much more formal than the colloquial diction of the hobbits. For example, translated, the Common Speech as the elves speak it is a language without the informality of contractions—elves say *cannot* rather than *can't*. The faintly archaic character resulting from this formality suggests the elves' racial age, for they are the firstborn who were created in the First Age, before men and dwarves came into the world. Thus for Elrond to speak of his "sire" or to "deem" a doom appropriately dates him. Similarly, Celeborn's observation that "Oft it may chance that old wives keep in memory word of things that once were needful for the wise to know" as much suggests a respect for the past, with his choice of words and the way he orders them, as with the sentiment he expresses. In this way Tolkien creates for the reader some sense of the degree of formality of the Sindarin, the Elvish tongue spoken in Middle-earth.

The vocabulary of the elves is easily perceived as the most musical of the languages of Middle-earth, largely because of the high proportion of liquids (*l*'s and *r*'s) and of vowels that are sounded in the front of the mouth. These features give the language a quickness and sparkle that is accentuated by the tendency of Elvish words to be polysyllabic and to feature sequences of unaccented syllables. As Tolkien describes the language in the appendices, "Where the last syllable but one contains (as often) a short vowel followed by only one (or no) consonant, the stress falls on the syllable before it, the third from the end." That is, words with pronunciation patterns like that of *slippery* or *listening* are prominent in the language, and the characteristic linking of unaccented syllables gives the language the impression of speed.

The pure musicality of the language he had in-

vented was one of its chief charms for Tolkien, who
saw how the shapes and sounds of even an unknown
language could work on the imagination to produce
images and effects. It is the same phenomenon that
leads people to say that the word *Schenectady* sounds
like a railway switching yard. The connection is not at
all a matter of meaning; it is purely one of the suggestion of the sounds. And this is the phenomenon
Frodo experiences as he listens to the music of Rivendell for the first time:

> At first the beauty of the melodies and the interwoven
> words in the Elven-tongue, even though he understood
> them little, held him in a spell, as soon as he began to attend
> to them. Almost it seemed that the words took shape, and
> visions of far lands and bright things that he had never yet
> imagined opened out before him.

Indeed, the speech of the elves abounds in those
effects that we generally call *musical*—a repetition
of vowel and consonant sounds, and use of onomato-
poeia in words such as *sighing* and *whispering.*

Another musical language of Middle-earth,
though one in which the tempo is much slower, is
Entish. The language of the Ents is characterized by
the translator as "slow, sonorous, aglomerated, re-
petitive, indeed long-winded; formed of a multi-
plicity of vowel shades and distinctions of tone and
quality." It is a perfect expression of the being and
character of a race that prides itself on never being
"over-hasty." The sonority and the agglomeration
and repetition are clearly reflected in the Entish version of the Common Speech that Fangorn speaks.
The long-windedness by comparison with the speech
of other races is perhaps best suggested by the very
long lines of the song Fangorn sings as he carries the
two hobbits through his forest: "In the willow-meads
of Tasarinan I walked in the Spring." The fifteen

syllable lines of this song are exceeded in length only by the sixteen syllable lines of the war song the Ents sing on their way to Isengard: "To Isengard! Though Isengard be ringed and barred with doors of stone." The line lengths alone illustrate the translator's assertion that Ents are "indeed long-winded."

As the languages of various races distinguish among them, the languages of various "nations" distinguish among men. Most distinctive are the men of Rohan, who speak a language that seems to be derived from Old English. John Tinkler has shown how many of the untranslated words spoken by the men of Rohan could be Old English words. For example, he suggests that *Éothéod*, reported by the translator to be the earliest name for the people of Rohan, is a combination of *eoh* (Old English "horse") and *theod* (Old English "nation or people").[13] Similarly, the names of Théoden's and Éomer's swords are Old English names: Théoden's *Herugrim* is in Old English "very fierce, cruel, sharp" and Éomer's *Guthwine* is "friend in battle."[14]

The translator also notes that when the hobbits first heard the men of Rohan speak, they thought they could understand or recognize a few of the words here and there. That is, their relation to the language of Rohan is about what ours would be to the language of a long lost colony of Anglo-Saxons. Yet the language is not inaccessible to the reader who lacks a knowledge of Old English. Our understanding of the importance of horses to the men of Rohan and the ubiquitous presence of the prefix *Eo* in Éomer, Éomund, Éowyn, Éored, Eothain, coupled with Gimli's first epithet to Éomer, "horse-master," is enough to suggest the etymology Tolkien was illustrating for us. Similarly, one need not know that the Old English *mearh* means "horse" or "steed" to see the meaning of the Rohan word *mearas* when it occurs in

context: "That is Shadowfax. He is the chief of the
Mearas, lords of horses."

As the men of Rohan resemble Anglo-Saxons in
language, they resemble them in culture. They are a
race in which the heroic code takes precedence over
all else, who "love war and valour as things good in
themselves, both a sport and an end." They sing of
past greatness in terms of "the helm and the hauberk"
and the old songs that celebrate the old heroes. And
Théoden's joy in being recalled to himself after years
of being undermined by Grima (Wormtongue) is not,
as we might expect, a song of rebirth in nature, but a
call to battle: "Arise now, arise, Riders of Théoden!"
Indeed, there is little in the songs of the Rohirrim to
suggest any relationship with the world beyond a
constant and heroic struggle to maintain life.

The men of Gondor and others of the
Númenórean line have in common with the Rohirrim
a gravity and an old-fashioned way of speaking that
suggests their high origins as well as their antiquity.
But unlike the Rohirrim, they celebrate "more skills
and knowledge than only the craft of weapons and
slaying." The songs of Gondor not only celebrate the
past, but preserve the wisdom of it, even beyond the
recognition of learned men of the present generation, as for example in the rhyme about *athelas*.

That the old songs of Gondor should preserve
wisdom beyond the understanding of the present
generation is fully appropriate, because the city itself,
like the Stewards who rule it, is the last preserve of the
strength and wisdom of the Númenóreans, the Men
of the West. And, as Faramir's observation on the
differences between Gondor and Rohan suggests, it is
important that the two rhymes of Gondor, the *athelas*
rhyme and Boromir's riddle, "Seek for the Sword
that was broken," both focus on a reawakening process without celebrating the martial arts. Indeed this

difference in thematic concern points up the appropriateness of Éomer's observation that Boromir was
more like a man of the Mark than like a man of
Gondor.

Finally, there is the unique case of the language
of Tom Bombadil. Bombadil is "Master of wood,
water, and hill," "oldest and fatherless," and will be
"last as he was First." He is a kind of Adam before the
fall, a natural man able to "sing" to all of nature, and a
link to the golden age. His status as a natural man is
reflected not only in his power over Old Man Willow
and Barrow-Wights, but also in his marriage to Goldberry, the River-daughter, who is described in terms
reminiscent of a water nymph: Her hair "ripples,"
and her gown is "green as young reeds."

Bombadil's songs are a mixture of nature imagery and nonsense. The nonsense lines with their
bouncy rhythm reflect the careless happiness of an
innocent nature, but Tom is not limited to this naive
role as his ability to sing control over Old Man Willow
and his stories of "evil things and good things, things
friendly and things unfriendly, cruel things and kind
things" shows.

The songs, and indeed Bombadil's normal discourse, are composed of lines which function either
as single units with heavy use of assonance and allit-
eration preserving the unity or as two-line units,
marked by strong caesura and rhymes. Whether the
basic unit is the single line or the couplet, each line is
marked by a strong caesura or midline pause. There
does not seem to be a pattern of number of syllables
or number of stresses before or after the pause, but
the pause itself is unmistakable, and links Bombadil
to the alliterative tradition in Old and Middle English
poetry, and by analogy, to the ancient cultural past of
Middle-earth (in contrast with the elves, who would
be more nearly analogous to the cultural past of, say,

Rome and the Latin language). Bombadil's lines fall naturally into two parts:

I had an errand there:	gathering water-lilies
green leaves and lilies white	to please my pretty lady,
the last ere the year's end	to keep them from the winter,
to flower by her pretty feet	till the snows are melted.

Not only do Bombadil's songs lead back to an historical past, his other utterances allude to a mythic past when the natural mode of discourse was song —this is another reference to the golden age when all of humankind and nature communicated. So Tom sends the hobbits to bed, saying,

Some things are ill to hear	when the world's in shadow.
Sleep till the morning light,	rest on the pillow!
Heed no nightly noise!	Fear no grey willow!

Bombadil's language and his use of it not only locate him morally by associating him with the other natural goods in the work, but also help to locate him historically and geographically in Middle-earth. He is thus one of the best examples of what it can mean to say *The Lord of the Rings* is philologically inspired.

In contrast to the lilt and flow of the language of the elves, the friendly informality of the hobbits' language, and the stateliness of the languages of Rohan and Gondor, the language of the Orcs, the Black Speech of Barad-dûr, looks and sounds dark and horrid: Its alien appearance is emphasized by its use of suffixes to mark grammatical function (dur-batuluk), its use of hyphenated forms (Saruman-glob), its jaw-breaking clusters of consonants (Uf-thak), and its frequent use of vowels that are pronounced with the tongue well back in the mouth (Lugburz, Nazgul).[15] The language looks and sounds as though it were cut out of wood, and so clicks and thuds into place instead of flowing.

When the translator writes in the appendices that "Orcs and Trolls spoke as they would, without love of words or things; and their language was actually more degraded and filthy than I have shown it," he directs our attention to the perversions of language reflected in the example of an Orc proverb, "Where there's a whip, there's a will, my slugs." He contrasts the Orcs' brutality and their tendency to see the world as covered with their own slime with the simple optimism and determination of the common "Where there's a will, there's a way" and the more grave and determined "Where will wants not, a way opens" of Rohan. In his note, the translator also recalls to us Shagrat's harangue: " 'Curse you, Snaga, you little maggot . . . he knifed me, the dung, . . . I'll put red maggot holes in your belly." To listen to Orcs talk is to hear a language that draws most of its imagery from the processes of death and decay.

The physical ugliness of the language, which mirrors the moral depravity it expresses, is represented by Tolkien's giving Orc speech, whether it is the Black Speech or the Orcish corruption of Westron, configurations and pronunciations that are unfamiliar and harsh to the eyes and ears of speakers of English. His two chief devices in creating a sense of the ugliness of the language are the use of clusters of consonants in combinations we find unusual and unpronounceable, such as the *zg* in "Nazgul" or the *bh* in "bubhosh," and the use of back vowels, vowel sounds that are made with the tongue pulled back in the mouth, such as the *u* in "buck" or the *o* in "glob." The combination of harsh consonants and back vowels makes the language sound harsh and grating, while the clustering of consonants in unusual combinations, the use of the circumflex and hyphenation of words ("Burzum-ishi" or "Saruman-glob") combine to make it look equally ungainly. If the Orcs can be said to have a culture, something of its nature as the antithesis of the orderly, the organic, the creative, and the worshipful can be perceived from the extraordinary ugliness of their language.

Thus, the language, and particularly the songs of Middle-earth, clearly serve to establish the uniqueness of each people of that world. Thematically and formally, they allude to a variety of languages and cultures from our world, from the Old English sparseness of the Rohirrim to the romantic ballads of the elves. However, the most formal and most elevated style is reserved for the great Eagle who brings the news of victory at the Dark Gate to the city of Gondor:

> Sing now, ye people of the Tower of Anor,
> for the realm of Sauron is ended for ever,
> and the Dark Tower is thrown down.

The reverberations of form and content here are biblical, with particular reference to the psalms. The image of a savior-king who will return to rule the faithful and the promise of a return to life by "the tree that was withered" have Christian reverberations that again reinforce the sense of elevation, the high importance of the song, as does the identity of the messenger, for in medieval Christian iconography, the eagle was the symbol of St. John the Evangelist, who is noted for his contemplation of the divine nature of Christ, and quoted for the opening line of his gospel, "In the beginning was the Word. . . ."

Thus, though it is possible and even practical for a reader with no particular philological background to comprehend and appreciate the uses to which Tolkien puts languages in *The Lord of the Rings,* it is by no means true that he "uses a remarkably plain variety of everyday midtwentieth century English."[16] In *The Lord of the Rings,* Tolkien used languages to delineate cultural attitudes, to expose racial personalities, and to lead the reader to an understanding of or a feeling for the quality of consciousness of the various groups. His achievement is that he did so without interrupting the flow of his epic story, without sacrificing action to exposition or character to stereotype.

4

⟳⟳⟳⟳⟳⟳⟳⟳⟳⟳⟳⟳⟳⟳⟳⟳⟳⟳⟳⟳⟳⟳

The Quest as Myth:
The Silmarillion

The Silmarillion, Tolkien's posthumously published account of the First Age of the world, is the densest, the most difficult, and for the general reader the least attractive of all his works. As a backdrop to *The Lord of the Rings* and *The Hobbit, The Silmarillion* is perhaps the most essential of Tolkien's works; at the same time it is the least able to stand alone as a unified vision. Although individual tales from this chronicle of the earliest age of Middle-earth may be exquisite, or majestic, or horrifying, *The Silmarillion* as a whole has neither unity of tone nor unity of style. In addition, the number of characters is simply staggering. So while *The Silmarillion* is Tolkien's most ambitious project, it is in many ways his most flawed performance.

Some of the difficulties of the work may be attributed to its unfinished state at the time of Tolkien's death and to his accretive method of composition. When he died in 1973, he was still reworking, redefining, and refining this mythology of his imaginative world. The book as it stands was edited by his son, Christopher, who selected and arranged materials from Tolkien's unpublished writings. He cites some of the obstacles to successful completion of the task in the foreword:

The Silmarillion was already in being half a century ago; and in battered notebooks extending back to 1917 can still be read the earliest versions, often hastily pencilled, of the central stories of the mythology. But it was never published . . . and throughout my father's long life he never abandoned it, nor ceased even in his last years to work on it. In all that time *The Silmarillion,* considered simply as a large narrative structure, underwent relatively little radical change; it became long ago a fixed tradition, and background to later writings. But it was far indeed from being a fixed text, and did not remain unchanged even in certain fundamental ideas concerning the nature of the world it portrays; while the same legends came to be retold in longer and shorter forms, and in different styles. As the years passed the changes and variants, both in detail and in larger perspectives, became so complex, so pervasive, and so many layered that a final and definitive version seemed unattainable.

From this account, it seems unlikely that Tolkien could have finished *The Silmarillion* under any circumstances, for its subject matter grew with him, changed as he changed, and evolved as he and the world outside his imagination evolved.

Like the poem *Beowulf,* which Tolkien studied and loved, *The Silmarillion* is not really a narrative in the sense that it tells a story in a straightforward and sequential manner. Instead, the collection of tales with its cross-references, modifications, and contradictions is presented as a mythology which, having come from divers hands and divers places, cannot be expected to achieve any great degree of inner consistency. The pose of the narrator, then, as a translator or as an editor obviates criticism of the lack of unity in the work.

To say, however, that *The Silmarillion* lacks narrative unity is not to say that it lacks structure. Indeed, the work is highly structured, taking the form of a triptych, a three-paneled picture often used as an altarpiece. This structure seems to have been part of Tolkien's own plan for the work, for Christopher Tolkien notes in the Foreword that the first and third panels "are included according to my father's explicit intention."

The large central section, the *Quenta Silmarillion,* or "History of the Silmarils," is flanked on one side by the story of the creation in the *Ainulindalë* and the *Valaquenta,* and on the other by the story of the decline of the elves and the rise of men in the *Akallabêth* and *Of the Rings of Power and the Third Age.* As in an actual triptych, the central panel is the largest and carries the most meaning, but the two side panels provide a context for the central panel, give a perspective on it, and direct the eye toward it. The relative emphasis to be placed on the three panels is a function not only of size but of orientation, for the central panel is focused straight ahead and so seems independent, while the side panels make connections with the central panel and defer to it. Thus by placement of the parts and by proportion, *The Silmarillion* is an account of the history of the elves of Middle-earth. It is, at the same time, a symbolic representation of the fall of man because it is in the nature of myths to link gods, demigods, and men.

In *The Silmarillion* the two most important influences in Tolkien's life came into direct opposition: his religion and his love for the ancient and heroic north. On the one hand, his philologist's mind told him that the mythology of the ancient Britons must be similar in most ways to other northern mythologies.[1] On the other hand, as much as he loved those mythologies, and as much as he celebrated the heroes of the unbendable will, he was a Christian and thus could not rid his mind utterly of the notion that this life is but a prelude to another. *The Silmarillion* thus reflects a mythology that combines the values of the unconquerable will with the certainty that whatever the outcome of the temporal battle between good and evil, the last battle is yet to come.

A mythology, it is said, is a public dream. If a people find themselves frightened of a nature they can neither understand nor control, troubled by the fear that their human enemies are stronger and more skillful in warfare than they, and longing for the protection of some greater and stronger force against both nature and men, it is not to be wondered at that they dream of a golden age when all of nature communicated, when men were like gods, and when mighty heroes crossed seas or galaxies to aid them in their struggles. And if men dream of such golden ages, it is also not to be wondered at that they consider how man declined from that blessed state. In his mythology for England, Tolkien dreams both of these dreams.

As a hopeful mythmaker, Tolkien has two possibilities: His work may describe the harmonious existence of the world after the end, or it may focus on the unharmonious times between the beginning and the end. For Tolkien, the choice is clear; as he wrote in *The Hobbit*, ". . . things that are good to have and days that are good to spend are soon told about, and not much to listen to; while things that are uncomfortable, palpitating, and even gruesome, may make a good tale, and take a deal of telling anyway." The emphasis will be on the decline of the world from the golden age.

The first panel of the triptych, which depicts the creation of the universe, begins with the assumption of a single, ruling, creative force: "There was Eru, the

One, who in Arda is called Ilúvatar." In describing
Eru and the creation, Tolkien uses the familiar notion of a world that is built to music and is, therefore,
ideally "harmonious." He is quick to establish a tone
which aspires to the heroic through the use of unusual words (Arda, Ilúvatar); extensive use of formal
sentence structures such as parallelism ("And he
spoke . . . ; and they sang . . . ; and he was glad"); and
the use of words associated with religious teaching
("Brethren," "the Void," "and it came to pass"). The
combination of heroic tone and religious connotation
identifies *The Silmarillion* as mythic. It also helps Tolkien to establish the ultimately hopeful nature of his
work. Even in the first panel, as he raises the specter
of the long trials that will comprise the central portion of the work, Tolkien evokes the splendor and the
glory of the first conception of the world by the
Ainur. Then he quickly notes, "Never since have the
Ainur made any music like to this music, though it has
been said that a greater still shall be made before
Ilúvatar by the choirs of the Ainur and the Children
of Ilúvatar after the end of days. Then the themes of
Ilúvatar shall be played aright." That is, Tolkien immediately asserts without equivocation an eschatological vision of harmony: There will be an end to this
world, and after that end perfection will once more
be attained. But until that time, the music will be less
than perfect. The vision of harmony after the end is
one that Tolkien attributed to early Christians in
Briton, and one that stands in dramatic contrast to
the stark hopelessness of the more ancient northern
mythologies. Thus, though he has created a mythology for England in *The Silmarillion,* he was providing
it from the beginning with a Christian element. This
mythology was to be like ancient northern mythologies in its tone and its constant awareness of the
threat of chaos, but unlike them in its hopefulness.

Presented with the fact of Ilúvatar in the opening lines, the reader is not hesitant to accept the pronouncement of the One that "no theme may be played that hath not its uttermost source in me." That is, because everything in the world, including the great source of evil, Melkor, is created by the One, his understanding must exceed all other understanding. And whatever Melkor attempts to do by way of rebellion against the One will be bent, finally, to the achievement of Ilúvatar's ends, though Melkor's limitations of vision may not let him see how this is possible. This is not, certainly, to say that everything that happens in Tolkien's world is for the good. Tolkien's view is more nearly akin to Alexander Pope's "All partial evil, universal good" with its assertion that evil does exist but that there is a plan to the universe and every occurrence somehow tends toward the end predestined in that plan.

Like the *Ainulindalë,* the *Valaquenta* is at once foreboding and hopeful. As a narrative it is remarkably weak, for it simply focuses on each of the Valar in turn, describing their powers and their responsibilities—Ulmo is Lord of the Waters; Aulë is Lord of all the substances of which the earth is made; and so on. It is a catalogue of characters, not a story. But though the *Valaquenta* tells no story, it heightens the sense of impending disaster at the same time as it encourages the careful reader to look ahead with hope. The sense of foreboding grows by virtue of the organization of the *Valaquenta.* Evil, introduced under the heading "Of the Enemies," is given the position of power: Morgoth and Sauron are introduced last, so that the section closes with an evocation of the darkness, suffering, and treachery they will visit upon Middle-earth.

While the foreboding engendered by the *Valaquenta* is a function of its structure, the hope it holds out is a function of its language, for Tolkien uses shifts in tense to distinguish what continues to be from what has ceased to exist. The Valar, with the exception of Morgoth, are all described in the present tense: "The Lords of the Valar are seven; and the Valier, the Queens of the Valar, are seven also." Of Manwë he writes, "Sulimo he is surnamed, Lord of the Breath of Arda," and he continues, "Ulmo is the Lord of the Waters. He is alone." But the descriptions of Morgoth and Sauron are consistently put in the past tense. Of Sauron, the narrator says, ". . . in after years he rose like a shadow of Morgoth and a ghost of his malice, and walked behind him on the same ruinous path down into the void." Here then is the promise of the *Valaquenta,* expressed through its language: Morgoth and Sauron, violent, tyrannical, and cruel, will pass from the world, and the Valar who love the earth will endure.

As the overall structure of *The Silmarillion* is architecturally tidy, so is that of the central panel. The *Quenta Silmarillion* has twenty-four books; elves dominate the whole but are the exclusive subjects of the first half (men do not even appear until chapter 12). In the second half the *Quenta Silmarillion* develops the connection between elves and men and depicts the ultimate combining of the blood of the two kindreds in the greatest hero of the First Age, Eärendil the Mariner.

The *Quenta Silmarillion* is therefore not only the history of the Silmarils, but of the elves as well. In addition, the Ainulindalë and the *Valaquenta* are assumed to be derived from elvish sources, as the narrator finishes the tale of the creation in the *Ainulindalë,* for example, by noting that "it is told among the Eldar" how the Valar fought Morgoth before the coming of the elves. Similarly, the Akallabêth and *Of the Rings of Power and the Third Age* come from elvish sources. Although nothing suggests that the world of men ended when the last ships sailed from the gray havens, the tale ends when there are no longer any elves in Middle-earth through whose eyes it may be seen, and when the last vestiges of a world different and more heroic than our own have vanished.

Clearly, then, the elves are at the center of *The Silmarillion*. But although the tales that comprise *The Silmarillion* are primarily tales of elves, the narrative voice is not itself elvish. The speaker stands outside the time of the elves and, though he knows the tales and the histories, he knows them as a scholar or a descendant, not as a participant. The narrator can tell what happened in the creation, loss, and recovery of the Silmarils, not because he was witness to the mythic events he describes, but because he has inherited the stories of them. His distance in time is suggested by his repeated allusions to lost tales of the Eldar in utterances such as "It has been told" and "[the tale] which is full told in that lay is called *Narn i Him Húrin*."

Although the title of *The Silmarillion* suggests that the fate of the jewels draws the unnamed narrator to the tales of the elves, such does not actually seem to be the case, for many of the episodes have little direct connection with the jewels. Rather, the Silmarils are primarily important as the means by which elves and men become estranged from the Valar and thus from the One. The tales are unified not so much by the jewels as by the theme of the struggle against Morgoth, that personification of malice, greed, and destruction that is the evil side of the heroic life. Morgoth's hatred of men and elves predates the creation of the Silmarils, and his malice, as personified by his servant Sauron, survives their irretrievable loss and, indeed, his own disappearance

from the world. Thematically, *The Silmarillion* is first
concerned with the undying, yet hopeless, struggle of
man against evil and the inevitable decline of the
children of the earth.

As long as the Eldar are content to accept the
gifts of the Valar and Ilúvatar, they are innocent and
protected. But in Fëanor comes the kind of knowledge that contributes both to the rise and to the
decline of man. On the one hand, it makes men more
nearly the equal of those beings they call gods; on the
other, by destroying their innocence, it cuts them off
from the protection they enjoyed in the unified world
of the golden age. Fëanor's original name, *Curufinwë*,
contains the root *skill* (curu); *Fëanor* itself means *spirit
of fire*. From skill and spirit Fëanor brings to the
Eldar, among other gifts, the letters "which the Eldar
used ever after." Thus Fëanor, as *spirit of fire* is a
culture hero like Prometheus. And as was true of
Prometheus, his gift to his race is double-natured: It
is an *ipso facto* blessing, but it is also the cause of great
misery. Panofsky wrote in *Studies in Iconology,* "The
torch of Prometheus lighted at the wheels of the sun's
chariot . . ., carries the 'celestial fire' which stands for
the 'clarity of knowledge infused into the heart of the
ignorant'; and . . . this very clarity can only be attained at the expense of happiness and peace of
mind."[2] Fëanor's knowledge, like that of Prometheus, is gained at the cost of the happiness and
peace of mind of the whole race.

Fëanor's rebellion and his transgression of the
assumed law of Arda, obedience to one's betters, is an
elvish fall from grace, analogous to the fall of Adam
and Eve in the garden of Eden. When, like Adam and
Eve, elves must leave the garden, a messenger appears at the very edge of the guarded realm to deliver
"the Doom of the Noldor": "Tears unnumbered ye
shall shed; and the Valar will fence Valinor against

you, and shut you out, so that not even the echo of
your lamentation shall pass over the mountains."

The doom of the Noldor dominates the *Quenta
Silmarillion* as, chapter by chapter, noble aspirations
are thwarted, noble motives are misunderstood,
noble men and elves are needlessly killed or maimed.
As it was true in *The Lord of the Rings* that a power for
evil could not be used in the cause of good, it is true in
The Silmarillion that the disobedience of the elves
turns everything they do to ill ends. So strong is the
doom of the Noldor that it even reaches out to cor-
rupt the lives of men who come after the elves.

Men, the second race, thus become a representation of the further deterioration of mankind in the
ancient past. Elves are no longer innocent and care-
free; after the fall they are given to plots and rages,
despondency and violence. They lose their spiritual
superiority to man as we know him. With the appearance of the race of men, we see that the mythic race
will lose its physical superiority as well: Men are
weaker, shorter-lived, less quick with mind and
tongue and hand than elves.

Because of the pride and disobedience of the
elves as symbolized in Fëanor, the world of the *Quenta
Silmarillion* is a vale of tears. From Fëanor,
the mightiest of the Noldor; to Turgon, once abandoned by Fëanor on the ice; to Beren One-hand; to
Túrin Turambar; the heroes of elves and men suffer
physically and spiritually under the formidable assault of evil on Middle-earth. The recurrence of the
torture of heroes in *The Silmarillion* points out the
hopelessness of their earthly lives. The succession of
disasters visited upon Túrin Turambar, for example,
nearly exceeds even the bounds of the tragic: He
banishes himself, kills his best friend, makes an incestuous marriage with his sister, and, reacting in anger
and disbelief to the revelation of the truth, kills the

bearer of the bad news. His suicide, by which he acknowledges the final victory of despair, shows for the first time how death may come as a blessing from Ilúvatar.

Tolkien's achievement in the creation of Turambar is that he has at once created a mythic representation of man at the mercy of the banal evil of earthly life—the kind of evil that is devastating because it does not discriminate between the good and the bad, but afflicts all alike—and a consistent fictional character whose intemperate responses always result in disaster. Túrin becomes a symbol in the course of his undeserved suffering at the hands of the world, but he also remains a believable character with his recurrent lapses of self-control and ensuing repentences.

For all the suffering it recounts, the *Quenta Silmarillion* concludes with hope. After twenty-three chapters chronicling the failure of heroes to transcend the doom of the Noldor, the twenty-fourth, "Of the Voyage of Eärendil and the War of Wrath," tells of the forgiveness of the Valar and the return of divine mercy and pity to Middle-earth. Here Eärendil is a hero in the most mythic and the most religious sense: He is someone who saves us. In doing so, he not only secures the pardon of the Valar, he also succeeds in returning the elves to the west. Further, Morgoth is banished into the Void. Yet the world cannot be remade and the seeds of evil are still fertile even though Morgoth himself is destroyed. The tone suggests, however, that the victory is partial and temporary, for the language is mournful and slow: "Here ends the SILMARILLION. If it has passed from the high and the beautiful to darkness and ruin, that was of old the fate of Arda Marred; and if any change shall come and the Marring be amended, Manwë and Varda may know; but they have not revealed it, and it is not declared in the dooms of Mandos."

The most important theme of the *Quenta Sil-marillion* is the decline of mankind. The second most important is the union of opposites. As the tone is both foreboding and hopeful, as Eärendil is both man and elf, the Two Trees of Valinor also combine opposites. The Two Trees, the sources of the light of the Silmarils, are born from the green mound called Ezellohar, called forth by the song of Yavanna and the tears of Nienna. Yavanna is the giver of fruits, the lover of all things that grow. Nienna is the mourner: She mourns for the marring of the world by Morgoth and for those who wait in the halls of Mandos, i.e., those who are dead. From the moment of origin, then, the Two Trees and the light they literally shed on the ground of Valinor is made up of generation and decay, of growth and decline, of birth and death.

Like the sun and the moon with which they are readily identified, the Two Trees follow a natural cycle in which one waxes as the other wanes: "Thus in Valinor twice every day there came a gentle hour of softer light when both trees were faint and their gold and silver beams were mingled." In the image of the Two Trees is a celebration of the golden age when the opposites of nature were unified rather than separate. Night is not separate from day, nor youth from age, nor male from female. Instead we have the paradoxical situation in which each quality or being maintains its individual character without being separated from its opposite. This perfect independence within perfect interdependence is a reflection of the paradoxical relationship of free will and predestination that is so important to Tolkien's ideas about the possibility of heroism.

Furthermore, for a Christian, the Two Trees of Valinor must suggest two other trees that have their own paradoxical relationships: the tree of knowledge of good and evil (i.e., of man's fall) and the cross, the tree of life (i.e., of man's redemption). Certainly the

Two Trees of *The Silmarillion* are connected with the
tree of knowledge of good and evil, for it is to immor-
talize their light that Fëanor seeks and uses knowledge in creating the Silmarils. In a sense, the jewels
are the fruits of the tree, and it is the disposition of
the fruits that results in the Noldor's leaving their
"garden" of Valinor and going into the world where
evil has easy access to them and where they carry the
propensity to evil with them.

The fruit of the second Christian tree, the tree of
man's redemption, is Christ, and there are powerful
parallels between this convention and Tolkien's
handling of the Silmarils. Like Christ, one of the
Silmarils becomes a symbol of hope in Middle-earth
as it lights Eärendil's way through the heavens. The
parallel is emphasized by the narrator's observation
that, once lost from Middle-earth, the Silmarils will
not be regained (i.e., come again) until "the world be
broken and remade," or until the end of the world.
Finally, like the cross itself, the White Tree of
Númenor, called Galathilion and descended from
Telperion, is a symbol throughout *The Silmarillion*
(and in *The Lord of the Rings*) of man's faithfulness to
the Valar and to the elves, and a symbol of the love
and concern the Valar and the elves bear men.

Finally, the Silmarils, like Christ, serve as a symbolic link between the spiritual and physical worlds,
the realm of the Valar and the world of men and
elves. Determined and self-sacrificing as he is,
Eärendil cannot find the straight road to the west, the
spiritual world, until he receives a Silmaril to light the
way. It is the symbol of grace that allows men and
elves to transcend the bounds of the mundane world.
When the first Silmaril reaches its rest, bound to the
brow of Eärendil, disposition of the two remaining
Silmarils indicates the approaching equilibrium in
The Silmarillion. The host of Valinor comes to the aid

of Middle-earth, Morgoth is vanquished, the two remaining Silmarils are recovered from the Iron
Crown and seem destined to return to Valinor with
the victors. However, Fëanor's oath again exerts control, and his two remaining sons demand the jewels.
When Eönwë, messenger of Manwë, refuses,
Fëanor's sons steal the gems only to find that they
cannot bear to hold them. Maedhros, driven to despair by his inability to keep the oath that has driven
him through hundreds of years of anguish, throws
himself and his Silmaril into a burning chasm. Mag-
lor, the poet, casts his jewel into the sea and spends
the rest of his days in Middle-earth singing of pain
and regret on the shore. Thus, Fëanor's three jewels,
which began as symbols of the unity of creation, end
by emphasizing the separation of the material world
into its elements: earth, water, and air.

Although the dispersal of the Silmarils to the
elements establishes the equilibrium for which the
work has been striving by bringing an end to the oath
of Fëanor, the tone of "The Voyage of Eärendil" and
thus of the *Quenta Silmarillion* is not unequivocally
optimistic. Morgoth is defeated and evil is cast into
the Void: That much is hopeful. But the loss of the
Silmarils dominates the final pages, and the reader is
left with the sense of that loss and the sense of a world
disfigured.

The third panel of the triptych, the *Akallabêth* or
"Downfall of Númenor" and "Of the Rings of
Power," provides a coda to the central panel, a re-
capitulation of the theme performed by different
principals. Like the elves, the men of the three faithful houses are given a land of their own with every
promise of a blissful life. But, like the elves, they come
under the shadow—this time in the person of
Sauron. The freedom, or *free-doom,* of the men of
Númenor is reflected in the physical location of

Númenor itself; it rises out of the sea between Middle-earth and Valinor, symbolizing their position midway between the totally spiritual and the totally physical. As was the case with both Morgoth and Fëanor, the desire to approach the godlike drives men toward evil. When men cease to trust that the state of being to which they are assigned is the only one possible for them and begin instead to try to adopt the state of being of another race (in this case, to gain immortality), they take the first steps toward an alliance with Sauron. Eventually, their frustrated desire to sail into the west drives them into the hands of Sauron, the darkness that rises in the east.

As the *Akallabêth* and "Of the Rings of Power" trace the rising importance of men, they also track the progressive withdrawal of the elves from Middle-earth. In the *Akallabêth,* the elves who listen to the summons of the Valar withdraw from Middle-earth to the Isle of Eressëa, and the men of the three faithful houses depart to Númenor, also beyond the sea. With the destruction of Númenor, however, men known as Elf-friends return to Middle-earth and, with the descendants of men who had sided with Sauron and with the elves who had remained in Middle-earth, they again come into conflict with Sauron. His defeat by the "Last Alliance" of men and elves marks the end of the Second Age.

Like the two books that deal with the coming of the elves into the world, the books that tell of their parting are at once hopeful and filled with foreboding. The departure of the elves from Middle-earth is continually alluded to and used to evoke a state of loss. Without the presence of the elves, men are deprived of "good counsel and wise lore" and fall into the "Darkness." The beauty of elvish voices and elvish arts is withdrawn from the world, as is the memory of a time without evil. In the Third Age, the image of what the world of the elves was is preserved only by the power of the elven rings: one preserves Imladris or Rivendell; another Lothlórien; the third is hidden. When the destruction of the Ruling Ring ends the power of the three rings of the elves, the last traces of the Noldor pass out of the world.

At the same time, the destruction of the Ruling Ring achieves the final overthrow of Sauron. The greatest servant of evil is vanquished, and his final destruction marks a moment of rebirth as spring comes again to the earth. In the penultimate passage, renewal is the central image: "Peace came again," "a new Spring opened," "the glory of the Dúnedain was renewed," and "the White Tree flowered again." Though all of these events signal the passing of the elves, they also signal a beginning of a new cycle, the dominion of men.

The paradox of a pattern that is simultaneously linear and cyclical is expressed not only in Tolkien's use of the language of recurrence to record the passing of the elves but also in his conception of the structure of the world. In the flat world made for the children of Ilúvatar, the Ancient West was the home of wisdom and goodness. But when the Dúnedain attempt to sail straight into the west, they discover that for them the world is round. In the waning years of the elves, the world is paradoxically round and flat at the same time, as the final image of *The Silmarillion* suggests: "In the twilight of autumn [the ship of Círdan] sailed out of Mithlond, until the seas of the Bent World fell away beneath it, and the winds of the round sky troubled it no more, and borne upon the high airs above the mists of the world, it passing into the Ancient West."

As in the *Ainulindalë* and the *Valaquenta,* Tolkien maintains in the two closing books a careful distinction between the past, which furnishes the subject matter for the tale, and the present, which provides the perspective for the teller and for the reader. Present tense observations, for example, "As is told in the *Akallabêth*" and "as many songs have since sung," emphasize the teller's distance from the time about which he tells and at the same time lend authority to his telling.

The optimism of the work is, in part, a function of this placement of the narrator in ages long after the days of which he tells. As the *Quenta Silmarillion* suggests, to foresee the ultimate triumph of good over evil in the future is to rely on trust or faith; to comment on the present is to speak with far more assurance and with far more persuasion, as when the narrator of the *Akallabêth* tells how "Manwë put forth Morgoth and shut him beyond the World in the Void that is without; and he cannot return again into the World, present and visible, while the Lords of the West are still enthroned." Or when we read in "Of the Rings of Power" how ". . . towers [the Númenóreans] raised upon Emyn Beraid and upon Amon Sûl; and there remain many barrows and ruined works in those places, but the towers of Emyn Beraid still look towards the sea." These are observations that can only be made by those who come after the end of the age, years enough later to see the future become the past.

There are few movements of this sort which shift into the narrator's own time in *Akallabêth* and "Of the Rings of Power," and in each case the shift into the present tense lasts no more than a single sentence as opposed to the *Valaquenta* which is predominantly present tense. Although these time intrusions assume the continuity of the race of men, they are not sufficient to neutralize the elegiac quality of the books. As the last panel of the triptych, the two final books may tell of men, but they direct our gaze to the

passing of the elves, concluding with a poignant evocation of the end of a race, an age, a language, and a
literature: "And an end was come for the Eldar of
story and of song."

As the narrative quality of *The Silmarillion* resembles that of *Beowulf,* so does the strategy of the
poet. Tolkien has created in *The Silmarillion* the illusion of surveying a past that reaches back to a long
history of sorrow, one noble and fraught with great
significance. The recurrent allusions to lost tales
("The Lay of Leithian," "The Lay of Eärendil," and
"The Narsilion," most of which presumably exist in
other forms of the tales in *The Silmarillion*) serve to
create a sense of a past that must have been truly
heroic and noble to have given rise to so many heroic
tales. The recurrent references to source poems also
create the sense that the author is working in the
context of a widely known and well-accepted body
of literature—a living mythology. However, *The
Silmarillion* as we have it is not the mythology itself,
but a heroic, elegiac poem based on it. The poet's
wide acquaintance with and knowledge of this heroic
past allows him to see in the recurrent joyous creation
and sorrowful destruction something of permanent
value. He tells again the oldest of mythic tales, the
unending struggle of good against evil; he depicts
again the oldest of human tragedies, the inevitable
death and destruction of man and all his works; and
he balances the two possible responses to the inevitable end—the pagan and the Christian.

The pagan or pre-Christian eschatological view,
as Tolkien explained in his essay on *Beowulf,* is based
on "the creed of unyielding." In the northern
mythologies, at least, the heroic assumption was that
the destruction of man and his creations was inevitable. The creed of unyielding, then, holds that chaos
will eventually triumph and that, for that reason,

human life can be made meaningful only by opposing chaos with all one's strength and will until death inevitably comes. The heroic life may end, but the heroic will is indomitable.

The Christian response to the inevitable human death is, however, based upon a vision of a life after death. The battle between good and evil in this world only presages the great battle beyond the end of the world, when victory or defeat will finally be decided. As the physical life of man is transitory, it may end; but the spirit of man is immortal. Even the Apocalypse is but a prelude to the final battle, for the end of the world is part of the design of that world. The creed of unyielding, the central code of the heroic pagan, is transformed in the Christian to the creed of faith. The ability to modulate the creed of unyielding to the creed of faith is a central point of difference between the good and the evil of *The Silmarillion*.

The forces of evil in *The Silmarillion* are led by Morgoth and Sauron, both beings analogous to fallen angels, who were created by Ilúvatar in the time before Arda (the earth) was created. The Valar, of whom Morgoth is one, are the greater of the two orders of the Ainur, "and men have often called them gods." "Of the same order as the Valar but of less degree" are the Maiar, of whom Sauron is one. The Maiar are servants and helpers of the Valar and seldom appear to elves and men. The manifestation of evil in *The Silmarillion* is real enough and devastating enough when elves fight elves and men fight men, but such encounters are, even to modern men, items of local interest. The greater victories and more desperate defeats come in opposition to an enemy against whom resistance is at once hopeless and necessary. Morgoth and Sauron, greater in kind than men and elves, are that sort of enemy, as are their

allies and creations, Ungoliant, the gluttonous
spider, and the winged dragons. When the Valar, out
of pity for the plight of men and elves, march against
Morgoth, it is a spectacular victory of mercy over
justice; but when the elf/man Eärendil saves the host
of Valinor by slaying the winged dragon Morgoth has
loosed against them, when the lesser rises up to oppose the greater, that is heroism.

The concept of heroism in *The Silmarillion* is far
more diffuse and ironic than in Tolkien's earlier
works. In contrast with *The Lord of the Rings,* which
provided heroes at every level of mimesis and at every
level of society, *The Silmarillion* seems to lack even one
unifying champion. Tolkien felt the lack of a single
hero and at one time proposed to provide the needed
continuity by framing the tales with a sea-farer to
whom all the stories could be told. However, the
sea-farer never materialized, and the continuity that
does exist comes from the enemies, Morgoth and
Sauron, rather than from the legions of elves and
men who oppose or resist them. *The Silmarillion*
shares this feature with another great collection of
myths, the Bible, in which a succession of heroes of
men all come to stand for one man who, in turn,
stands for all men. This, then, is the key to the
heroism of *The Silmarillion:* The heroes of the Valar,
of the elves, and of men are all aspects of one man
whose significance is universal, whose struggle is unending, and whose earthly fate is never in doubt. The
defeat in time and in the world is inescapable; the
dream of an ultimate victory is unforgettable.

The highest and only undefeated power of *The
Silmarillion* is Eru, the one, also called Ilúvatar. It is he
who creates the Valar and from whose thought they
create Arda, "the Realm." It is also he who creates
elves and men, and who decrees that the Valar are to
be "chiefs" rather than "gods" to them. It is he alone

who knows the fate of the world after the end of all
the ages. Finally, it is he who knows and understands
how the great design is unified, how everything has
its origin in himself and contributes to his own
greater glory.

In this conception of the One, Tolkien has
clearly created a source of good like the Christian god
and one which embodies the same paradoxes. For
example, he is the source of all creation and yet is not
responsible for the presence of evil. He knows what
will occur (that is, he sees the whole "design") but he
does not will it. If Valar, elves, and men cannot understand why events unfold as they do, it is because
they do not see the design whole and thus cannot see
how every event is in accordance with the ultimate
plan of Ilúvatar. He is, in short, all powerful and all
knowing, but also incomprehensible, and because he
represents a heroism we cannot understand, much
less hope to emulate, Ilúvatar is no more the hero of
The Silmarillion than Jehovah is the hero of the Old
Testament. For heroism as it is commonly understood, we must look to the lesser orders of beings.

Next in power below Ilúvatar are the Valar who,
inspired by the thought of the One, create Arda. In
them we see the first outlines of a comprehensible
heroism in *The Silmarillion,* for the Valar are the first
in Arda to oppose evil in the form of Morgoth. The
heroism of the Valar is rooted in their determination
to realize the visions that come to them from the One.
Although they know that after the first assault on
Arda by Morgoth they cannot achieve the perfection
of the original vision, they persevere in their attempts
to bring the world they have imagined into being. In
doing so, they are creative, obedient to the will of Eru,
and loving toward their fellow creatures.

The allegiance of the Valar to the visions and the
rebellion of Morgoth against those visions both serve

to illustrate the free will of the race; that is, it suggests that obedience is a matter of choice, not of fate. According to traditional Christian thought, to choose freely to bend one's own will to that of a divine being is to choose to participate fully in the ultimate perfect order and joy. To choose to oppose that will is to choose pain and frustration, which means to choose to be in a state of sin. The naive ideal of obedience is illustrated in Aulë's willingness to destroy the dwarves he has created in clumsy imitation of the creativity of Ilúvatar: Aulë's willingness to act according to the will of Ilúvatar results in his being forgiven for overstepping his bounds and in his dwarves' being absorbed into the great design. Aulë with his dwarves and Yavanna with her trees are paradigms of the best relationship between creators and their creations. The responsibility they feel for the works of their hands and the affection they have for those works combine the best qualities of the Christian god and the pagan lord: mercy and a fierce protectiveness.

While the love of the Valar for their own creations is shown by the desire to protect them and yet to let them be free, the love of the Valar for elves and men is shown by their wish to identify with these "children of Ilúvatar." When the formless Valar assume the shape of elves so that they may walk among them without causing fear, they parallel the act of the god who assumes human form in order to emphasize his own humanity and, conversely, to illustrate man's divinity.

The Valar are mythic heroes in stature as they have supernatural powers: they are mythic in being as they are forces of nature. Each of them is associated with a realm of the natural world—earth, air, water. Although Tolkien was among those who rejected the idea that all myths are allegories of nature, he did not go so far as to suggest that the natural world has no influence on myth. Thus when he identifies the Valar with nature, Tolkien creates a fictional structure in which nature supports elves and men in their struggles against evil. When elves and men refuse to extend to the Valar the obedience that is due them as "chiefs" of men, nature and humanity are out of joint and man is estranged from nature.

The relationship between the Valar and Ilúvatar is fundamentally Christian in nature because, although the Valar love the world they create and their creations for the world, they also understand that beyond the realm of the earthly is the realm of Ilúvatar, and that even the marring of Arda accrues to the glory of the One. To the elves, however, the world is a darker place than it seems to the Valar. Their characteristic attitude toward the world is more nearly pagan, marked by an unwavering will and a strict adherence to the law of loyalty to the lord that is the core of the heroic pagan code. Once Fëanor refuses to subordinate his will to that of his natural leader ("chief"), the shortcomings of the heroic code become evident.

Among the elves, the greatest protagonists are Fëanor, maker of the Silmarils, and Turgon, Lord of Gondolin. However, the tragedy of the elves is that, thanks to the oath of Fëanor and the ensuing doom of the Noldor, they have only heroes whose actions bring catastrophic results. Allegiance to the code of the will can not bring victory; it can only bring, at best, glorious defeat.

Fëanor's claim to the status of hero depends upon his role in the two central events in the history of the elves: the invention of the Fëanorean alphabet, which the elves adopted exclusively and which, by implication, makes the tales of *The Silmarillion* available; and the creation of the Silmarils, the jewels upon which most of the history of the elves in

Middle-earth depends. Fëanor is not only a strong, swift, cunning, and brave physical hero, he is also a culture hero, responsible in large measure for the way the whole culture of the Noldor develops.

Fëanor shares with the Valar a desire to create, and as he is ". . . the most subtle in mind and most skilled in hand" of all the elves, he is so nearly godlike that his creations are nearly divine in their beauty. Unlike the Valar, however, Fëanor fails to respect the necessary freedom of all creations, including his own, and he fails to recognize or to accept responsibility for his fellow creatures. For example, the oath by which he binds his sons and followers to him effectively destroys the free will he should strive to enhance. In his desire to control others rather than to help them to be more fully themselves, he fails to be merciful or protective, or to discharge the responsibility of a leader.

In contrast to Aulë, who willingly though sorrowfully prepares to obey the command to the One, Fëanor defies the Valar by denying their right to ask him to sacrifice his creations, the Silmarils. His disobedience to his natural superiors results in a catastrophic sundering of the ties that bind families together, and, by analogy, those that bind nations and cultures. In addition, because the act of disobedience puts Fëanor and the Noldor in a state of sin, the doom of the Noldor must be construed to be an observation of what must naturally happen to those who indulge their own wills rather than a curse originating with the Valar. In this particular, the flight of the Noldor from Valinor also resembles the expulsion of Adam and Eve from the garden.

Turgon, the second great hero of the Noldor, is one who swore Fëanor's oath and defied the Valar with him. Betrayed by Fëanor and left to brave the ice fields of the Helcaraxë, he turns away from the oath-keepers and, at the urging of Ulmo, Lord of Waters, builds a hidden city. The city of Gondolin, "whose fame and glory is mightiest in song of all dwellings of the Elves in the Hither Lands," becomes the last refuge of the Noldor in Middle-earth, a city of bliss, beauty, and wisdom. But from the moment Turgon fails to repudiate the oath and his own will and make himself subject to the will of the Valar, the fall of Gondolin is foretold. That is, it too is part of the doom of the Noldor. The fall of the city is brought about by the same heroic flaw that drives Fëanor to his death: the overweening pride of the creator in his own creation. Having built his beautiful city, Turgon cannot leave it, although he remembers the warning of Ulmo: "Love not too well the work of thy hands and the devices of thy heart; and remember that the true hope of the Noldor lieth in the West." This is a clear warning against pride, and an exhortation to follow the Valar; the failure to heed it leads to the sacking of the city, the death of Turgon, and the end of the Noldor as a culture. Lacking a state of grace and a willingness to bend one's will to those naturally superior, such as the Valar, even a leader as strong, wise, and creative as Turgon cannot survive the relentless onslaught of evil.

Among the race of men, heroes suffer less because they transgress the rules of obedience and responsibility than because they are victims of a world that fails to reward action with justice. For men, the world visits evil on the just and unjust alike. And as men are frailer, shorter-lived, and more limited in understanding than elves, they are even more susceptible to the evil of the world and less able to believe that a greater power loves and protects them than the elves. The two greatest heroes of men who suffer the banal evil of an ironic world are Beren and Túrin.

Beren One-hand, whose story is told and retold in *The Lord of the Rings* as a paradigm of steadfast

commitment, here illustrates the hope for man's redemption in the world. The root of Beren's heroism
is in his enduring love for Lúthien and in his willingness to suffer and sacrifice for her. But the root of
his ultimate victory, the happy life with Lúthien, lies
in her willingness to sacrifice for him. The love between the two is not, at first glance, a love of the
creator for the created, but in a sense it is precisely
that. Love for Beren moves Lúthien to repudiate the
immortality of the elves for the mortality of men; thus
he re-creates her. And when her choice allows them
both to return to Middle-earth to live out a second life
for Beren, she has re-created him.

The tale of Beren and Lúthien is a dot of light in
the midst of the *Quenta Silmarillion*. Although the
language is as formal and elevated as that of the other
tales, the tone is lighter and holds out the faintest
promise of hope. The narrator introduces the tale by
alluding to its difference: "Among the tales of sorrow
and of ruin that come down to us from the darkness
of those days, there are yet some in which amid weep-
ing there is joy and under the shadow of death light
that endures." As hero of this somber and yet joyful
tale, Beren accumulates qualities of the fairy-tale
hero: He is, Thingol reminds him, infinitely inferior
to the princess whose hand he seeks; he sets out on a
quest for a token of his appropriateness as a suitor; he
is assisted by a supernatural helper, Huan the great
hound, who speaks to the lovers three times. Yet, any
trace of triviality is removed by the high seriousness
of the tone, by the tortures Beren endures, and by the
defeat he suffers, which can only be made into victory
by the transforming power of love. Beren's story
reaffirms our belief that although earthly battles
must end in defeat, the last battle still offers hope.

By contrast, the tale of Túrin Turambar, far
from preserving joy and light, evokes only unrelieved
suffering and unmitigated pain. The tale is an anom-

aly in *The Silmarillion,* because only in this instance
does Tolkien develop character in such a way as to
make events seem to occur as a result of one's interac-
tion with the world rather than simply as the result of
evil. Túrin is a strong and capable warrior, but he is
quick to anger and nearly irrational in the face of real
or imagined insults. With the antagonism of Morgoth
pursuing men, he never lacks cause for irrationality.
At first Túrin's violent and unthinking responses
seem meaningless in themselves, unless they serve to
illustrate the meaninglessness of life in a world that
can visit constant punishment on one flawed man.
But when Túrin finally understands that his one
happiness, his marriage, is incestuous and thus runs
on his sword in remorse, we see for the first time how
death may truly be a gift to mankind.

In the tale of Túrin Turambar, as in all the tales
of men and elves, we see heroic impulses and heroic
men twisted in their attempts to save themselves,
their people, and their cultures. When one man is
saved from physical pain or spiritual isolation, it is
never by his own skill or cleverness: Such beings as
these are ultimately powerless against the pervasive
and elemental evil of a Morgoth or a Sauron. Though
elves and men are brave and skillful, they can only be
saved by love (of a Lúthien for a Beren, or an
Eärendil for the two kindreds) or by mercy (of the
Valar for the two races). And love and mercy are the
qualities that define the one genuine hero of *The
Silmarillion,* Eärendil the Mariner.

Significantly, Eärendil is a representative of both
men and elves, being the son of Tuor (a man) and
Idril Celebrindal, daughter of Turgon (an elf). As a
representative of both races, he can ask pity for both
races. His determination to sail into the west signifies
his love for men and elves and his willingness to
sacrifice his own life for them. The sacrificial nature

of his voyage is suggested by his response when the
Valar rule that he, his wife, and their two sons shall
each have the right to choose to which of the races
their fates shall be joined. Like Frodo, Eärendil has,
through his sacrifice, moved beyond earthly concerns. He directs Elwing, "Choose thou, for now I am
weary of the world."

As a rescuer of mankind, Eärendil shares important characteristics with other culture heroes. He is,
assuredly, mortal, but he is also half man, half elf, at
once the descendant of the house of Huor and of the
house of Finwë. His dual nature is emphasized by the
choice he is given to join his fate with men or elves and
by the choices his sons make: Elros chooses to go with
men and become the first King of Númenor; Elrond
chooses to go with the elves and live in Middle-earth
until the end of the Third Age as the Master of
Rivendell.

Eärendil is archetypical in the service he per-
forms for the two kindred, too. Although he is physically brave and skilled enough to be the warrior-hero
(he alone kills the winged dragon that is Morgoth's
last defense), his great contribution is to ask for
mercy and pity for elves and men. To secure the pity
of the Valar, he is willing to sacrifice his own life.
Further, having succeeded in his attempt to intervene
on behalf of men and elves, he does not return to live
among them as a hero; rather he remains separate
from them and, viewed from afar, becomes a symbol
of hope.

In the heroic figures of *The Silmarillion,* two
modes of conduct are consistently reflected—the
creative and the sacrificial. The creative, in Morgoth
and Fëanor in particular, is of necessity associated
with the life-force, with the expansion of the hero's
being. But among the subtle and skillful creators the
joy of creation is replaced by the joy of control. The

mind that perceives creations as possessions instead of creatures with wills and beings of their own is a mind that attempts to gain by power what can only be freely given. There is, then, a lack of respect for the hierarchical principle of willing allegiance to one's betters.

As Morgoth and Fëanor are characters who demonstrate the effects of a lack of fealty, Aulë, creator of the dwarves, illustrates that life-giving creativity and fealty may exist together. Like Morgoth and Fëanor, Aluë creates his creatures and comes to love them. But he perceives that the allegiance he owes his own creator is of the first importance. Significantly, while he is the only creator in the work who is willing to sacrifice his creations in the name of trust in and allegiance to his "lord," he is also the only one who is not responsible for the loss or destruction of his own creations. Paradoxically, in being willing to give up his creations, he earns the right to keep them. This is the paradox that has always been at the center of the sacrificial act and the essence of Tolkien's concept of heroism.

Among the most celebrated creations of *The Silmarillion* are the texts of the tales that make up the work itself. Here, as in *The Lord of the Rings,* Tolkien creates a narrator who is styled as the translator and editor of old texts. His knowledge of Elvish mythology is wide and deep, and his delight in the Elvish languages is apparent in the attention he gives them in his appendices and glossaries.

Tolkien's fascination with languages is, by now, no surprise. What is surprising in this work is the difficulty that fascination creates for the reader. Of *The Lord of the Rings* one could say without hesitation that the language themes were beautifully integrated with other thematic concerns; in fact in that work the themes and the language are perfectly suited to one another. However, the success of Tolkien's uses of

language in *The Silmarillion* is questionable. It can be
argued, as Jane Nitzsche has done, that Tolkien's
fascination with languages has made *The Silmarillion*
nearly unreadable: "A problem with this mythological work," she writes, "is its plethora of names of
peoples, individuals, and places (the 'Index of
Names' supplied by Christopher at the end list an
appalling eight to nine hundred, many of which are
mentioned only once . . .)."[3] However, having acknowledged the limits of Tolkien's use of the language theme in *The Silmarillion,* one may go on to
appreciate even a minor achievement. This "plethora
of names" is not simply the self-indulgence of an
aging writer; instead it is a major part of one of the
most important themes of the work, the centrality of
the creative impulse to human experience.

   Thematically, the naming and renaming that is
so prominent in these tales is a constant allusion to the
principle that to use language, particularly to name,
is to create. Impatience with *The Silmarillion* is often a
result of expecting it to be something it is not: a
well-plotted adventure story, say, like *The Hobbit* or
The Lord of the Rings. But *The Silmarillion* is not basically a narrative; it backtracks, modifies, contradicts,
and reconsiders far too often to be trying to tell a
single story. Rather, its purpose is to tell *stories* and, in
doing so, to evoke a feeling for a time, a culture, and a
set of values. The issue is not what becomes of
Fëanor, or even of Eärendil, but what becomes of
people (good and bad) when pride and envy and
blind fear conflict with humility and self-sacrifice. In
creating new versions of such universal myths, Tolkien maintains through his last work that the quintes-
sential human activity is creation, particularly linguistic creation.

   From the opening of the *Ainulindalë,* Tolkien
celebrates the centrality of song, the most elemental
use of language, to human activity. The creation of

the world by song identifies reality as subjective, determined as much by what is inside us as by what is
outside in the world. As we can only describe what we
imagine or what we imagine we see or hear or smell,
the act of imagining and then of describing becomes an act of creation. And as describing is an act of
language, the world is, in a sense, created by
language.

As the linguistic act is central to the creation of
Arda, the development of language is central to the
existence of the elves as a unique race among the
creatures of Arda, "For . . . they had met no other
living things that spoke or sang." The elves, in calling
themselves "Quendi, signifying those that speak with
voices," establish Tolkien's definition of humanity:
To be human is to be a user of language. By extension, the essence of humanity is creativity, for using
language well is the most creative activity in Tolkien's
world.

The creation of a written language among the
elves parallels the development of their speech and
further illuminates the importance of language in
The Silmarillion. By attributing the development of
the Fëanorean alphabet to the rebellious son of
Finwë, Tolkien suggests that the development of language, a Promethean step, can be both a blessing and
a curse. In perceiving the world around him, the user
of language also responds to his own creation, and in
responding to it, he defines himself as separate from
other parts of creation. It is not until the concept of
separation exists that one can exercise free will, because until a sense of separation exists there is nothing from which to be free. Language is a blessing
because it allows man to define and thus create his
world, and it is a curse because it brings him to the
consciousness that he is distinct, perhaps even iso-
lated, from the rest of his world. Both the blessing

and the curse are inherent in the decision of the elves to call themselves "Quendi."

The further importance of language to a sense of self and to the survival of a culture is depicted in the separation of the Quendi into the Vanyar, the Noldor, and the Teleri. The Noldor retain the original language of the elves, Quenya, but the largest group of the Teleri become speakers of Sindarin, for, "by that long sojourn apart . . . was caused the sundering of their speech from that of the Vanyar and the Noldor." Quenya and Sindarin then develop separately until the return of the Noldor to Middle-earth at the rebellion of Fëanor. When Thingol, king of the Sindar, learns of the treacherous slaying of the Teleri during that flight and of Fëanor's theft of the white ships, he bans the language of the Noldor from his realm. This prohibition is the beginning of the destruction of the Noldor as a culture, and finally Quenya is only a "language of lore," not a language of living men. The doom of the Noldor, that all their works must perish, applies to the language as well as to cities and crowns.

Benjamin Whorf, a great American linguist, once wrote, ". . . every language is a vast pattern system in which are culturally ordained the forms and categories by which the personality not only communicates, but also analyzes nature, notices or neglects types of relationships and phenomena, channels his reasoning, and builds the house of his consciousness."[4] Tolkien's gift as a student of language was that he could look through a language to see that consciousness behind it. In *The Lord of the Rings* and *The Silmarillion,* his achievement as an artist is that he has helped his reader to see as he sees: first to look at the language and then to look through it.

The Silmarillion, then, is the story of a world that is too dangerous and unforgiving to be comic; it is also

the story of a world that is far too capricious, far too
capable of rewarding even the good with ashes, to be
really tragic. Instead, Tolkien here portrays a world
that is ironic: Danger is everywhere, villains may be
banished but not vanquished, the longed-for apple is
rotten at the core. The inhabitants of this world live
lives in which conventional notions of relations between actions and rewards are exploded. They live
lives in which the odds against good winning over evil
are almost absurdly high. However, caught in this
trap between high odds and bad bets, Tolkien's
heroes do the most heroic thing ironic heroes can do:
They endure.

In the tradition of heroic literature, Tolkien
takes pains to make his antagonists worthy opponents
for his beleaguered heroes, for if the battle against
evil is to have any meaning, evil must be capable of
winning. Morgoth and Sauron, had they not been the
greatest of evils, could have been among the greatest
of goods. Thus the elegiac tone of *The Silmarillion*
reflects not only the passing of a great age but also a
particularly poignant sense of heroic possibilities un-
realized. The nature of those possibilities, and the
causes of their failure to be realized, provide thematic
texture for *The Silmarillion* and suggest that Tolkien's
own world view was one that appreciated and longed
for the heroic, while doubting the possibility of its
triumph in the temporal world.

5

~~~~~~

The Quest Realized:
Secondary Worlds

Fairy stories and the ancient northern myths were constantly at the center of Tolkien's consciousness, providing the subject matter for his scholarly essays and the form for his imaginative writing. It is not accurate or even helpful to suggest that the two sides of Tolkien's life were separated. True, he was an Oxford scholar of genius who revolutionized *Beowulf* criticism and set a standard for unifying language study and literary study that has seldom been met. Charles Nicol wrote of him, "Words meant something different to him than to the rest of us: they were multilayered objects through which he could detect the pentimento of an earlier world, and the brilliance of his scholarship lay in his ability to reconstruct the milieu of a Middle English romance through a subtle analysis of its vocabulary."[1] At the same time he was a fantasist capable of creating a new world, complete and consistent in every detail. Although he cannot really be said to have revolutionized the writing of fantasy, he did catch the imagination of a whole generation of readers of many nationalities and cultural backgrounds. Detractors who want to dismiss him as a "cult hero" fail to realize that he was not simply the fair-haired boy of the antiwar movement in the United States. Something more than anti-Vietnam adulation is needed to explain translation of *The Lord of the Rings* into fifteen foreign languages, including Polish (1961), Japanese (1972), Hebrew (in preparation), and Spanish (in preparation).

Even if we remain at our most conservative and do not use the word *genius,* it is clear that Tolkien was an extremely successful practitioner of the critical and creative arts. He was also a skillful and perceptive blender of the two, always willing to use the skills and insights he had developed in one area to enrich his work in the other. Through this process of reciprocal enrichment he unified the two sides of his life as he always hoped the schools would unify the two sides of his subject: literature and language. In his valedictory address to the University of Oxford he said, "I have the hatred of apartheid in my bones; and most of all I detest the segregation of Language and Literature. I do not care which of them you think White."[2]

Tolkien's short stories, particularly when read with an eye to the circumstances surrounding their creation, provide clear examples of the way the two strands of his life twined together. Take, for example, the very early "Farmer Giles of Ham." It was written in the early 1930s, probably before *The Hobbit* was completed, for it shares certain narrative weaknesses with that work. After the first book's success, Tolkien offered "Farmer Giles" to Unwin, but as it lacked hobbits, it was set aside for a time. During the next year, Tolkien was asked to give a talk on fairy tales to the students of Worcester College. Procrastinating until it was too late to prepare a lecture, Tolkien decided to revise "Farmer Giles" and to read it as an illustration of his ideas about fairy tales. Worried about the reception he and his story could expect, he was amused and astonished by the behavior of his audience; he wrote of it, "The audience was apparently not bored—indeed they were generally convulsed with mirth."[3]

Like *The Lord of the Rings,* "Farmer Giles" may be said to be linguistic in inspiration, for the core of the story is the place-name Worminghall, a village near Oxford. Worminghall means dragon-hall or reptile-hall, and "Farmer Giles of Ham" is the story of an unwilling hero, Farmer Giles, and his confrontation with a marauding dragon, Chrysophylax, the worm in question.

In the Foreword to the story, Tolkien assumes the role of translator, as he did so often in later works, to observe that "Farmer Giles" is a legendary account of the origin of the Little Kingdom, whose confines, he observes, are vague, but which seems to occupy the area we now call Oxfordshire and Buckinghamshire.[4] According to the translator, the title of the Latin manuscript from which the tale is taken is "The Rise and Wonderful Adventure of Farmer Giles, Lord of Tame, Count of Worminghall and King of the Little Kingdom." Much of the humor of this very funny story results from similar juxtapositions of the grandiose and the ordinary.

The hero of the story, Ægidius Ahenobarbus Julius Agricola de Hammo, or Farmer Giles, is awakened from a sound sleep one night by his dog, Garm, who warns him of an intruding giant. A blast from Giles' blunderbuss, mistaken by the giant for an attack by stinging insects, turns him away. The King of the Middle Kingdom sends Giles a testimonial and a long sword in thanks. When a dragon enters the Little Kingdom, Giles' sword jumps out of its sheath and is revealed to be the famous sword Caudimordex, or in the vulgar tongue, Tailbiter, the bane of dragons. Giles cows the dragon and accepts his offer of a treasure in exchange for his life. When the King of the Middle Kingdom tries to appropriate the treasure, Giles and the dragon join forces to keep it in the Little Kingdom, of which Giles eventually becomes King.

Like Bilbo and Frodo, Giles is an unwilling hero, and his unwillingness lasts throughout the story. But he is pragmatic, too. He doesn't really want to fight a giant, but "property is property." When the dragon appears, his response is similar. It is only the scorn of the miller, the support of. the parson, and some strong ale that persuades Farmer Giles to ride out to do battle with the dragon. Even when he is persuaded to go, he remains unheroic: His armor is an old leather jerkin with iron rings stitched to it; his helmet is covered by his old hat; and his steed is his old gray mare. Even Chrysophylax comments on his short-comings as a hero, saying, "It used, sir, to be the custom of knights to issue a challenge in such cases, after a proper exchange of titles and credentials."

However, the real knights of the Middle King-dom are even less heroic than Giles. They are effete, interested only in the forms of knighthood, the proper fashions, the order of precedence, and the innate inferiority of everything provincial. They are probably no braver than Giles (who never claims to be brave) and they are certainly much less prudent, as they sing and jingle their way to the dragon's cave and are decimated by his surprise attack on them. Though Giles knows the forms, he isn't inclined to follow them.

Despite his reluctance to fight giants and dragons, Farmer Giles is a traditional fairy-tale hero. His heroic attributes are not obvious or conven-tional—he is not braver or stronger, or wiser, or more handsome than other men—but he is a hero nonethe-less. What virtues he has are, like Bilbo's, the virtues of the powerless: prudence (in loading his blunder-buss and in covering his ring mail with a cloak), dis-cretion (in agreeing to leave part of the treasure for Chrysophylax in return for the dragon's protection), and reverence for the past (in his appreciation of Tailbiter). However, as the narrator notes, his most important characteristics are luck and wits. Like traditional fairy tales, "Farmer Giles of Ham" suggests that, with these two qualities, what appears to be a perfectly ordinary person might well be a real prince.

As a prince, and later as a king, Giles illustrates what the function of a ruler really is. The loss of the Middle Kingdom, which includes the loss of the King Augustus Bonifacius, is no loss at all, for in that Kingdom the greater (the King and his knights) use the lesser (the farmers) without being useful to them. The falseness of the court's mode of conduct is symbolized by the practice of using a confectionary dragon's tail to replace the real tail that was traditionally eaten on Christmas day. Cake and almond paste and scales of hard sugar icing are a measure of how far King Augustus Bonifacius and his knights are from the ideal of the days of Bellomarius and Caudimordex. On the other hand, though he never masters "Book-Latin," Giles creates a court that is "respectable," which means it is a court in which merit is rewarded as the advancement of the twelve likely lads shows.

Structurally, "Farmer Giles of Ham" also imitates the traditional fairy tale. Giles has three trials (the giant, the dragon in the kingdom, and the dragon in the mountains) through which he is drawn progressively outward into the world. First he drives the giant off his own farm; then he meets the dragon in the neighboring village; finally, he pursues the dragon "north-west to the walls of Wales." Having pursued evil to its source, Giles achieves the end that Sam hoped for Frodo in *The Lord of the Rings*. Unlike Frodo, however, Giles can go home to enjoy the life he has preserved in Ham. His reward, seen in contrast to Frodo's, again points up the difference between the comic world of fairy tales and the more tragic vision of *The Lord of the Rings.*

As fairy tales are often concerned with the progress of the individual, they generally resolve with some symbolic representation of the hero's advance into responsible adulthood. Again "Farmer Giles" is typical. Giles begins as Bilbo did, concerned primarily with filling his stomach and preserving his own property. His adventures, however, prepare him for rewards that will call upon him to take a more mature, less self-centered view of his duties. He is disqualified from one traditional fairy-tale reward, marriage, because he already has a wife who becomes "good Queen Agatha." However, to be made Lord of Tame, and eventually King of the Little Kingdom is, ideally, to assume a responsible familial role that denotes maturity. Being king, he becomes responsible for his friends and neighbors and works for their benefit all of his life, as befits a good ruler.

Despite its inherent morality, "Farmer Giles of Ham" is clearly intended more to entertain than to teach, and both its tone and its intent are comic. Tolkien has a little fun at the expense of a great many kinds of people and institutions: He creates an unhelpful narrator who writes an unhelpful scholarly preface for the tale; he creates a king, August Bonifacius, whose name means "doer of good" but who does no good; he parodies and parallels *Sir Gawain and the Green Knight* and *Beowulf,* the two poems with which he has been most concerned professionally, by adapting episodes in those heroic tales to fit his own low-mimetic hero. He also has a little fun at the expense of linguists who research the origins of place-names and attempt to draw conclusions about the events through which they came into being.

Perhaps the most interesting of all Tolkien's parodies in "Farmer Giles of Ham" is his parody of himself. By the time "Farmer Giles" was published in 1949, Tolkien had published *The Hobbit* and finished *The Lord of the Rings*. The parallels are too numerous to be individually acknowledged, but one can generalize that "Farmer Giles" presents situations from the two longer works as they would have occurred in a gentler, more accommodating world. For example, in *The Hobbit* one of the most important episodes is the descent of Bilbo into the dragon's tunnel; in "Farmer Giles" the old gray mare worries about what will happen if Giles has to go into the dragon's lair, but luckily he doesn't. The dragon obligingly goes in and brings the treasure out for him.

"Farmer Giles of Ham" is connected to *The Hobbit* and *The Lord of the Rings* not only by the reworking of situations, but also by Tolkien's awareness of and thoughtful use of language. He makes perfectly terrible puns in "Farmer Giles," as when he observes that Giles' dog Garm couldn't even speak dog-Latin, or when he names a do-nothing king Augustus Dogood. He indicates his affection for the ancient Britons over the Latin-speaking invaders by having the farmers, who get the best of it, speak the vernacular, and he marks the vernacular with a countrified lexicon ("yammering," "Lord-a-mercy," "Tailbiter"). He establishes the writer of the original manuscript as one of the learned by having him refer to the tongue of the farmers as "the vulgar tongue." As in *The Hobbit*, the most elegant language is used by those who oppose the hero—especially Chrysophylax and the King, both of whom use formal diction to mask their devious intentions. An exception is the parson, who, though his language is learned, is a hero in his own way. He is treated in much the same fashion as Gandalf was treated in *The Hobbit*. Though he is the leader who succeeds in setting an unwilling hero in motion, he is also the object of fun, as when the narrator observes the perfidy of Chrysophylax:

". . . if this regrettable lack in one of the imperial lineage was beyond the comprehension of the simple, at least the parson with his book-learning might have guessed it."

Finally, the study of language itself is the object of humor: The parson should be able to "see further into the future than others" because he is a grammarian. The compilers of the *Oxford English Dictionary* are described as the "Four Wise Clerks of Oxenford" who defined a blunderbuss as "a short gun with a large bore firing many balls or slugs, and capable of doing execution within a limited range without exact aim. (Now superceded in civilized countries by other firearms.)" And, in fact, the *OED* does define it that way. Tolkien seems to have been greatly amused by this definition, not the least by the suggestion that improved firearms are an indication of an advanced civilization.

"Farmer Giles of Ham," then, is in many ways typical of Tolkien's work, especially in its use of traditional structures, in its faintly medieval flavor, and in its interest in language. But in other ways, it is atypical; like *The Hobbit* with which it is coeval. "Farmer Giles" catches Tolkien in a narrative stance that he never assumed after 1938. It catches him using an intrusive narrator and thus destroying the seamless web of his story. How Tolkien came to reject this narrative strategy is explained in another instance of his combining his scholarly and imaginative worlds.

In the academies of the western world, it may still be held that Tolkien's most important nonfiction was the essay, "*Beowulf:* The Monsters and the Critics," which changed the course of critical thought about that Anglo-Saxon poem. But art is long and criticism is fleeting, and what seems to be an indispensable critical insight today is dismissed as a misunderstanding born of cultural limitations tomorrow. That is part of the nature of criticism. For the readers of Tolkien's fantasies, however, his most important work of nonfiction is, and will probably continue to be, the Andrew Lang lecture, "On Fairy-Stories," first delivered at the University of St. Andrews in 1938 and reprinted in 1964 in a volume titled *Tree and Leaf.*

As I suggested earlier, in developing this lecture, which was delivered in the year following the publication of *The Hobbit,* Tolkien discovered that some of the decisions he had made about *The Hobbit* and about "Farmer Giles of Ham" were not necessarily implied by the form he had chosen. He discovered, that is, that fairy-stories do not necessarily imply a child reader, so he did not have to provide a guide to steer his readers through such narrative devices as flashbacks. He discovered that he no longer believed that the teller of a fairy-story could undercut the reality of his own story. And he discovered that, for him, the fairy-story, unlike the traditional fairy tale, could include high-mimetic heroes—gods and demigods and godlike men—the stuff of myths and legends.

However, the most important concept Tolkien developed in his thinking about fairy-stories is the concept he called "sub-creation." Sub-creation, in his view, is essential to the success of a fairy-story. When a writer achieves sub-creation, Tolkien says, "He makes a Secondary World which your mind can enter. Inside it, what he relates is 'true': it accords with the laws of that world. You therefore believe it, while you are, as it were, inside." That is, the secondary world must have its own inner consistency: If the secondary world is like our primary world, except that the laws of gravity do not hold, then all of the natural laws of the primary world that depend upon the laws of gravity must also be adjusted. No gravity, for example, means that apples will not necessarily fall down—they may fall up or sideways or not fall at all, depending upon which way the wind blows. The point, however, is simply that the reader must never feel that the natural laws (or indeed, the social or psychological laws) governing the secondary world are simply imposed in order to create special effects. The secondary world must be as consistent and as interconnected as tree and leaf.

In Tolkien's view stories in which the author has achieved authentic sub-creation and in which the author has succeeded in creating a secondary world are paramount among works of literature in offering the reader *fantasy, recovery, escape, and consolation*. On these five concepts hang his conception of the nature and function of fairy-stories.

Fantasy, says Tolkien, embraces "both the Sub-creative Art in itself and a quality of strangeness and wonder in the Expression." Fantasy does not change the nature of the world in which we live, but it creates a world in which we could live. That is, it creates a world in which the physical laws, though giving rise to the strange and the wonderful, are coherent and understandable. Tolkien hastens to point out that fantasy and delusion are not the same; one becomes a fantasist not by ignoring reality but by being acutely aware of it. As *nonsense* of the sort written by Lewis Carroll or Edward Lear cannot exist separate from the notion of *sense* (logic), fantasy cannot exist separate from the notion of reality. The human mind, to use Tolkien's own metaphor, is a prism through which "the refracted Light / . . . is splintered from a single White / to many hues, and endlessly combined / in living shapes that move from mind to mind." The "many hues" are contained in the white light of reality, but the art of the fantasist is required to make them visible. The fairy-story, then, is a natural result of the human proclivity to respond creatively to the world it perceives.

For the writer and the reader of fairy-stories, the encounter with fantasy gives rise to *recovery, escape, and consolation*. By *recovery* Tolkien means "regaining a clear view." Here he avoids taking issue with the phenomenologists, refusing to say that in recovery we see things as they *are,* but settling for the assertion that we see things "as we were meant to see them." What he seems to be driving at here is the notion that fantasy, by putting the familiar in an unfamiliar light, helps us to see it as if we were seeing it for the first time. Thus, instead of saying, "That's a tulip" and dismissing the flower without ever being fully conscious of it, in *recovery* one looks at it flower, leaf, and bulb.

By *escape* Tolkien means more than the momentary loss of awareness of our present state, though he does not belittle that; he argues, "Why should a man be scorned if, finding himself in prison, he tries to get out and go home? Or if, when he cannot do so, he thinks and talks about other topics than jailers and prison-walls?" The metaphor here is telling: Tolkien sees man, in this essay, as *estranged* from a better world, as being, in fact, in prison. So when fairy-stories deny that man is separated from all the rest of nature, or when they deny that the doom of man alone is death, or when they create a secondary world in which man sees "as he was meant to see," they provide the writer and the reader with an escape from the limitations of humanity and, perhaps, an imaginative return "home."

Finally, Tolkien asserts that fairy-stories offer "The Consolation of the Happy Ending." He coins a word to describe the happy ending—eucatastrophe (a good catastrophe)—and says of it, "The *eucatastrophic* tale is the true form of the fairy-tale, and its highest function." The happy ending, part of what we have in earlier chapters called the comic world view, is for Tolkien a repudiation of the possibility of a universal, final defeat. From this repudiation comes, in the best tales, a stab of joy as poignant and moving as sorrow.

In "Farmer Giles of .Ham," as in *The Hobbit,* Tolkien has created rich, imaginative tales, full of wit, amusing characters, and interesting events, in which the author is continually calling attention to the unreality of the story. When Sam and Frodo talk about being inside a continuing story in *The Lord of the Rings,* they are still both as firmly inside the secondary world of that work as is the story of Beren and Lúthien to which they refer. Therefore, the illusion of the secondary world is not disturbed; but when the avuncular narrator of *The Hobbit,* or the easily distracted author of "Farmer Giles of Ham," breaks in to comment, the effect is an intrusion of the primary world onto the world of the story, and the spell of fantasy is broken.

The unknown author of "Farmer Giles" is present throughout the story, from the first paragraph when he introduces his main character and himself: "There was more time then, and folk were fewer, so that most men were distinguished. However, those days are now over, so I will in what follows give the man his name shortly and in the vulgar form: he was Farmer Giles of Ham." Throughout the tale he wanders in and out, delivering helpful messages such as "I find no mention of [the giant's] name in the histories, but it does not matter," or the famous passage about the Four Wise Clerks of Oxenford and the blunderbuss quoted earlier.

In addition to allowing his narrator to disturb the world he has created, Tolkien also makes fun of his own magic. In *The Lord of the Rings,* written when his art was more firmly under control, he introduces several original races without ever suggesting or seeming to entertain the possibility that they are not real; his treatment of Ents is perhaps the best example. But in "Farmer Giles" he can't resist playing with the idea that dragons do not exist by having his dragons play with the idea that knights do not exist: " 'So knights are mythical' said the younger and less experienced dragons. 'We always thought so.' "

Through these practices, in "Farmer Giles of Ham" and *The Hobbit,* Tolkien undermines himself and precludes the successful creation of a secondary world. Without the secondary world in place, the reader cannot feel its strangeness and wonder; he feels himself outside looking in rather than inside looking around. And if the reader cannot move his feet out of his primary world, he cannot experience the recovery, escape, and consolation that the fairy-story has to offer.

All this does not, of course, mean that "Farmer Giles of Ham" and *The Hobbit* are failures as stories. They are both quite delightful, and "Farmer Giles" is often uproariously funny. But neither of them participates in what Tolkien later came to think of as "Faery." They are both fairy tales in the traditional sense without being fairy-stories as Tolkien uses the term.

Although Tolkien presented "Farmer Giles of Ham" as a lecture in 1938, the story did not appear in print until 1949. The first of his short tales to reach print was the much quieter and more serious "Leaf by Niggle," the story of an artist who wants to finish one picture of a great tree before he has to go "on a great journey," which symbolizes his death. The tale was written about the same time as "On Fairy-Stories," though it was not published until 1947, and it shows Tolkien putting into practice the principles he enunciated in the essay.[5] The story was later reprinted as a companion piece to the essay in the volume entitled *Tree and Leaf* in 1964. "Leaf by Niggle" is a prose poem in which Tolkien beautifully creates and uses a symbolic tree. The story's success is limited for some readers by the unusually overt didacticism of it.

"Leaf by Niggle" was called up, at least in part, by the decision of one of Tolkien's neighbors to have a large poplar tree destroyed. However, the central symbol of the story, the tree, becomes far more than an ecological symbol. The tree comes to symbolize the ideal that lies behind the physical appearance of the tree. Tolkien here has turned the phenomenological argument around and allowed that an independent reality exists without reference to human perception. From time to time, the story suggests, we may catch a glimpse of that reality through the tree.

In Niggle, Tolkien has created an artist as hero, but he is an artist hero curiously flawed. Niggle is a man of some real perception; he is able to see not only what he has created, but what the creation itself implies. The important quality in Niggle's painting is not simply that he creates a background for his tree, but that he discovers that background. That is, he does not paint the background because he *imagines* that it could exist, but because he *sees* that it does exist. In that sense, he is a visionary hero. At the same time, however, Niggle is extremely limited. He does not see the picture as a completed whole; he only catches glimpses of the background. And if his vision is imperfect, his execution is even more limited, for his depictions of the leaves are never quite what he had hoped, though his picture of the tree is "quite unique in its way."

Niggle, in short, is both heroic and nonheroic: a perceptive artist, but a little silly and inconsequential as well, as his name applies. He fits the mold of the

Tolkien hero in being helpful to others (Parish, for example) and in being self-sacrificing (he gives up his last chance to finish the picture in order to do his duty). But unlike the less ironic heroes, Eärendil, say, or Aragorn, Niggle resents the sacrifice. He is a flawed hero as he tries to complete the one picture that will give his life meaning before he sets off on his journey.

The great journey of Niggle from his home and his workshop to the workhouse is paralleled by the implied journey at the end, when Niggle sets off for the mountains. The commitment to good works and service to others that Niggle should have achieved at home, the application to the task and the discipline he lacks, are all learned in the workhouse. He also learns through recollection to appreciate his neighbor, Parish. Thus Niggle's journey, like Bilbo's in *The Hobbit,* brings him to maturity, though in Niggle's case the maturity is spiritual rather than physical.

As Niggle's tasks in the workhouse parallel his tasks at home (there he worked by fits and starts, in the workhouse he is forced to keep at it; there he resented Parish's presence, in the workhouse he longs for it) his two trees parallel one another. At home the tree was a created representation; in Niggle's Parish it is real. There it was unfinished; in Niggle's Parish it is complete. There it called up only glimpses of its context; in Niggle's Parish the context for it is complete.

If Niggle's tasks parallel and if his trees parallel, then it is only reasonable that his journeys would also parallel, and as in the case of the tree and the tasks, the second version of the journey is the more nearly perfect. Niggle's first journey, a journey from life to death, is a "long journey" which is "distasteful" to him. He knows it is inevitable, but he dreads it and prefers not to think about it. Furthermore, he thinks of his great tree as the one picture he wants to finish before the long journey. But as is too often the case, the journey begins unexpectedly, and Niggle is not really adequately prepared for it. As he has failed to put Parish's physical house in order, he has also failed to put his own spiritual house in order.

The workhouse episode serves to make Niggle a more adequately prepared traveler. The conception of the workhouse is that it is a purgatory, a place of purification. The faults of character, the indecisiveness, the inability to apply oneself steadily, the resultant limitation of vision that accounts for the difference between leaves as he imagined them and leaves as he painted them, are overcome in the workhouse and in Niggle's Picture.

The purified Niggle, however, the Niggle who leaves the workhouse and experiences the perfect versions of his imperfect previous life in Niggle's Picture and Niggle's Parish, is prepared for yet another journey. The second journey takes him from a paradise we can imagine to what promises to be a good beyond our imagining. The paradise we can imagine is an earthly world made perfect. But "Leaf by Niggle" argues that beyond that is a joy and perfection we cannot imagine: Of the beauty and perfection of the mountains Niggle approaches in his second journey "only those can say who have climbed them."

Evil as a force in itself is not really an issue in "Leaf by Niggle." In his original form, Niggle is subject to error and imperfection, but he is not evil. Similarly, Parish, who can see only the natural world and not the artistically created secondary world, seems to be limited, but not evil. The nearest thing to evil is in the cool voice of Councillor Tompkins, who always wanted Niggle's house, used to "sneer at him while drinking his tea," and thinks that painting is useless. However, the ultimate end of both Niggle and Parish is beyond the reach of Tompkins or others of his type. They are, in the words of C. S. Lewis, "surprised by joy" in their world beyond the purgatorical workhouse where the mountains ring with their laughter.

The limitations that they must overcome are therefore a part of a lack of grace. The attainment of a state of grace, that is, of the state Niggle has achieved by the time he sets off for the mountains, cannot come about as a result of his own exertions. Niggle, and indeed any man, can work until his back seems broken; he can learn patience and discipline; and he can learn to forget the irritations and disappointments of the past. But he cannot lift himself out of the dark or open the shutters of his soul. That is a gift of grace, of the treatment of men according to the dictates of mercy and pity rather than those of justice.

Those who do not have grace, who exist in a fallen state, think they are living in an ironic world, a world in which we instinctively feel that the rewards are not properly matched to actions. For example, knowing that Niggle is an artist, we wince at the notion that he should have been expected to sacrifice his picture to repair Parish's roof. That he should be punished for failing to make that sacrifice seems at least unfair. Such a world fails to be whole, complete, and coherent for Niggle as it does for us. In it, he catches only glimpses of the world he will see steadily and whole when he has attained a state of grace.

In "Leaf by Niggle," then, the traditional fairy-tale hero and the fairy-tale structure are adapted to Tolkien's ideas about the fairy-story. The opening line, "There was once a little man called Niggle, who had a long journey to make," is a variant of the classic formula, "Once upon a time." As such, its virtue is, according to Tolkien, that it "produces at a stroke the sense of a great uncharted world of time." The town,

and indeed the world of "Leaf by Niggle," is
undefined in time and space, so there is no interfer-
ence of what we know with what Tolkien wishes us to
know. However, wherever and whenever Niggle
lives, his world is undisturbed by intrusions from our
primary world. The secondary world of the tale is full
and sufficient in itself.

The concept of recovery is also central to the
story, particularly in Niggle's first experience in the
land that comes to be known as Niggle's Parish and in
his first sight of his tree: "All the leaves he had ever
laboured at were there, as he had imagined them
rather than as he had made them; and there were
others that had only budded in his mind, and many
that might have budded, if only he had had time."
Here, he is seeing face-to-face and complete what he
caught in glimpses before. The experience of recovery is in itself part of the escape we find at the center
of "Leaf by Niggle," for it enacts the escape from the
limits of perception the primary world imposes on us.
At the same time the assumption of life at the other
end of Niggle's journey suggests an escape from the
fear of death.

In the most literal sense, Niggle's consolations in
the story are many: He discovers that his tree is real,
that he himself is a successful sub-creator; he discovers the *real* Parish behind the earthly imperfections
of a bad leg and a limited imagination; and he discovers the mystical unity of the world when he perceives
that he and Parish and the tree are all connected, all
part of the same creation. That discovery, revealed in
the Porters' naming their world "Niggle's Parish," is
the *eucatastrophe,* the happy turn that leaves the two
laughing until "the Mountains rang with it."

A systematic description of the fairy-story qualities of "Leaf by Niggle" makes it sound as if Tolkien
sat down with the list of rules for such tales and built

one the way a carpenter would build a house from a set of blueprints. But the reader of the story soon perceives that "Leaf by Niggle" is far too allusive and subtle a story to be written from a simplistic plan. In reading it, the reader is drawn into Niggle's world until he, too, feels the joy of the happy turn and perhaps catches a glimpse of a mountain before he puts the tale aside.

Though "Leaf by Niggle" contains no direct reference to religion, not even as much as *The Lord of the Rings* or *The Silmarillion* which at least contain references to "The One," it is plainly a story that reflects a deeply religious turn of mind. That is, while the story is not *about* Christianity, it celebrates certain Christian values: responsibility for one's neighbor ("houses come first" is a limited and legalistic version of "love thy neighbor"); the replacement of justice by mercy (the First Voice suggests the Old Testament God of justice while the Second Voice suggests the New Testament Christ of mercy); and the importance of grace over works. Most telling, however, is the clarity of vision Niggle experiences in the country of Niggle's picture; one who reads of his perception of ground and grass and, finally, the tree, cannot help but recall the promise of *1 Corinthians*, "For now we see through a glass darkly; but then face to face."

The values and attitudes "Leaf by Niggle" share with Christianity do not, of course, suggest that the story is a religious allegory. The story is not about God; it is about an artist whose ability to be a sub-creator means that parallels exist between him and the creator of the universe. Further, his desire to be a sub-creator, Tolkien suggests, implies the existence of that creator. "We make," he wrote, "in our measure and in our derivative mode, because we are made: and not only made, but made in the image and likeness of a Maker."

"Smith of Wootton Major," written in 1965–66, is the last and most fully realized of Tolkien's short tales. The characters are symbolic rather than individualistic, but the balance between theme and story is preserved beautifully, and Tolkien's instinct for allowing action to convey meaning wins over the desire to teach he demonstrated in "Leaf by Niggle." Like "Farmer Giles of Ham" and "Leaf by Niggle," "Smith of Wootton Major" originated in the difficulties arising from a critical task. In 1965 Tolkien was asked to write a preface for a new edition of George Macdonald's *The Golden Key*. In the preface he wanted to explain to the children who would be the readers of the new edition the meaning of the term *fairy*. As he began to explain how stories, characters, and situations of fairy are handed down through the centuries, surviving even though they are mixed with other inappropriate (nonfairy) elements, he caught himself slipping into a metaphor: "This could be put into a short story like this," he wrote. "There was once a cook, and he thought of making a cake for a children's party. His chief notion was that it must be very sweet. . . ."[6] Within a short time, the brief explanation had become a story, "The Great Cake," later "Smith of Wootton Major." The publisher had to make do without a preface for *The Golden Key,* and the intended reflections on the nature of fairy must be inferred from the haunting story that Tolkien wrote instead.

In discussing "Smith of Wootton Major" Tolkien insisted, as he did of all his other compositions, that "there is no 'religion' in the story," but he also allowed that "the Master Cook and the Great Hall, etc. are a (somewhat satirical) allegory of the village-church and village parson: its functions steadily decaying and losing all touch with the 'arts', into mere eating and drinking—the last trace of anything 'other' being left to the children."[7] The "other," of course, is the fairy element, for "Smith" is about fairy (Tolkien spells it *faery* throughout the story), and its importance in the life of the artist.

The reader soon senses that "Smith of Wootton Major," though it participates in faery, is no typical fairy tale. First, the tone signals immediately that the comic spirit does not prevail in Smith's world. There is a meditative quality to this story, generated chiefly by the shift in balance between representation and description in Tolkien's art. For example, when the elven warriors march up from the sea singing their victory song, no song appears: The warriors are "terrible" and the song is victorious, but they are simply asserted to be so or described as being so. Neither mariners nor song are represented, and the resultant lack of images that appeal to the senses heightens the somber tone of the passage.

The two gifts Smith brings back from faery suggest a second important difference between this tale and the traditional fairy tale. The archetypal fairy tale is built around groups of three; three little pigs, three attempts to climb the glass mountain, three journeys up the bean-stalk. There is a feeling of progress and thus of movement about this triple structure. But Smith's story falls into two blocks, a structure that is solid and strong, but static. The first block culminates in his dance with the Faery-Queen, from which he returns as "a giant"; the second culminates in his return from faery for the last time, when he and we are first conscious of him as an old man. Tolkien carefully parallels the two scenes in order to increase our awareness of the contrast between Smith as a young hero at the peak of his powers and Smith as an old man nearing the end of his life.

From the dance with the Faery-Queen, Smith returns alone with a flower in his hair; it is visible to all, and people recognize him as a hero and stare at him in wonder. At this moment he is the typical fairy-tale hero. From the second encounter he returns with a guide, Alf, unseen and uncelebrated, to give up the symbol of his heroic role. At this moment he is the hero at the end of his cycle, the dying king of myth. This basic contrast is elaborated by other parallels between the scenes. After the first experience, he is greeted by his whole family and drawn into a room to which he brings light. After giving up the star he is met by his son alone and drawn into a dark room which must be lighted by candles. From the dance with the Faery-Queen, Smith brings a "natural" flower that, being from faery, lives forever in its moment of perfection; from the second encounter he brings a flowerlike bell, a work of art preserving nature, that keeps only the memory of faery alive.

The treatment of the hero is a third difference between this tale and the traditional fairy tale, and it is one of the sources of the unusual tone and the sense of loss we feel as readers. Instead of a series of adventures leading to the hero's attaining and demonstrating maturity and competence, this tale looks to the end of the heroic cycle. It is a story of the hero's sacrificial death and the importance of the sacrifice to the community that remains. In Smith's case, for example, the sacrificial yielding of the star ensures that renewal will take place (in the person of Tim) and thus that the role of the artist will continue to be filled. The consolation for the reader, then, lies in the affirmation of continuity implicit in Smith's willing sacrifice and Tim's joyous, though unknowing, acceptance of it.

As it is symbolic of the artist's life, Smith's life suggests first that the ability to enter fully the world of faery is, as Niggle said, "a gift." Second, it suggests that the gift does not offer or even suggest an imaginative experience limited to the "sweet" or the trivial. The experience of faery is the clear vision of the world of Wootton Major: What is beautiful, good, and true in Wootton Major is even more beautiful, good, and true in faery. And what is dangerous or evil is more dangerous and evil. Smith sees weapons in faery, for example, that could make him first among armorers in his world, but he is wise enough and good enough to stay away from them. Instead, he brings back from faery the Living Flower, incarnation of the promise that the world of faery is immortal, and the silver bells, symbol of the ability of art to evoke the memory of faery, even in those not blessed with a star.

Finally, Smith's life suggests that although the artist's creations are immortal, his gift is transitory. In time he will lose the ability to enter faery and will seek what consolation he can find in home, family, work, the memory of the enchanted realm and the certainty of its immortality. The magnitude of Smith's, the artist's, loss combines with Tim's and the world's gain to give "Smith of Wootton Major" that blend of joy and sorrow that makes it unique among the short fairy-stories.

By virtue of his name alone, Smith is a low-mimetic hero, an everyman. As a child he was not at all extraordinary; even on the day of the Twenty-four Feast when he gave the trinket he found in his cake to Nell, who had found nothing in hers, he was only "one of the boys." Although this act of kindness and natural chivalry might suggest that he is special, there is no affirmation of his specialness until, on the morning of his tenth birthday, he awakens to sing a song of faery. Designated as his by his grandfather, the star is not so much earned by Smith's charity toward Nell as it is given, for faery, like grace, cannot be earned.

As an inspired artist, Smith creates objects that are, like faery, both useful and beautiful: The most homely objects made at his smithy have "a grace about them, being shapely in their kinds, good to handle and to look at," while those made for their beauty take "forms that looked as light and delicate as a spray of leaves and blossom, but kept the stern strength of iron." For Tolkien, the difference between the true artist and the false is the difference between the smith and the cook. While Smith can hold in his mind and his art two contraries (use and beauty, strength and delicacy), the cook's art is based on simplification and a concern for appearance over substance. What he knows about children is that they like fairies and sweets, and when he comes to make the all important Great Cake, he devotes most of his thought to how it should be decorated before discovering, to his surprise, that he has no idea what goes into the cake itself. His art is an art that fails to move beyond surfaces. Even when he meets faery face-to-face when Alf reveals himself as king, Nokes' limited imagination keeps him from seeing anything more than an "artful fraud." Even so, faery has a reality of its own and is quite beyond Nokes' influence. Though he believes not at all that the star is of faery, and though he mixes it up with toys, trinkets, and triviality, the star retains its magic and works its wonder on Smith's imagination and his art.

Through his journeys to faery, Smith learns that faery is not only not trivial, but that it is a "perilous realm" and is not to be treated carelessly. Inside faery, art and nature are united, as they are in Smith's art. Nature is in art and art is in nature, as exemplified in the image of the King's Tree: "Tower upon tower, into the sky, and its light was like the sun at noon; and it bore at once leaves and flowers and fruits uncounted, and not one was the same as any that grew on the Tree." But nature and natural cycles must include death and decay as well as growth and regeneration, so faery also contains frightening visions: elven warriors returning from battle; a glass-like lake with flames and frightening creatures in its depths; a roaring wind "like a great beast" that nearly kills Smith. Faery is, in short, beautiful and terrible, dangerous and hospitable, tragic and joyous, and above all, serious.

The most powerful symbol of the union of joy and tragedy in faery is the Faery-Queen. As an incarnation of the joyful she appears as "a young maiden with flowing hair and a kilted skirt" who instructs Smith in the perfection of the idyllic side of faery: "Then they danced together, and for a while he knew what it was to have the swiftness and the power and the joy to accompany her." As the incarnation of the tragic, the Faery-Queen appears "in her majesty and glory," crowned with a white flame. At this second meeting she instructs Smith in the pain of the tragic side of faery, the inevitability of loss.

Like the Faery-Queen, the King also embodies both worlds, and in doing so, he embodies both levels of heroism, the low mimetic and the high. Alf, the Master Cook's apprentice, is the king. He is ageless, which means simultaneously old and young. He is also simultaneously king and apprentice, ruler and ruled. His name, Alf, is both a familiar British nickname and an Old Norse form of *elf;* that is, it is both of the world of Wootton Major and of the world of faery.

The character of Alf also carries most of the burden for the most exciting theme of "Smith of Wootton Major," the interpenetration of worlds. Smith, the artist, enters faery, a transaction we understand as something like flying on wings of inspiration. But equally important is the penetration of faery into Wootton Major. Smith figures in this movement to some degree—he brings back gifts from faery—but most of the good that flows from faery comes from Alf, first as Prentice, then as Master Cook.

First and foremost, the function of a cook is to nourish. Alf comes out of faery to nourish in the sense of revitalizing the world's appreciation of imaginative creation. At a time when "too many had become like Nokes" life becomes progressively poorer and less satisfying as the appreciation of faery declines. But as Alf nourishes and replenishes by identifying and protecting the star, by baking the cakes, by refilling the spice box, and by repainting and reglazing the hall, we see that although its greatest effect is on the artist, faery affects the lives of all people. The revitalization of faery means the revitalization of traditions and institutions (the spice box and the hall) and the progress of humanity (the beautiful and lively children). Even a skeptic like Nokes profits from it, though he is too blind to see how.

However, the Faery-Queen assures Smith that even Nokes has some slight memory of faery. Thus the ability to perceive it is not so much a matter of consciousness as it is of degree. An awakening of perception is required: Once that has taken place one "sees" the world differently, that is, catches a glimpse of faery.

The Smith's ability to see the simultaneous worlds of Wootton Major and of faery, and the image of Smith as Starbrow, link him with the greatest Tolkien hero, Eärendil. As Eärendil could find the straight road to the west only after he bound the Silmaril to his brow, Smith can find his way to faery only after the star is affixed to his forehead. And the same will be true for Tim. Like Niggle's tree, the star is "a gift" both literally and figuratively.

Smith and Tim are different from the others then, not in kind but in degree. Smith looks about at the Twenty-four Feast and sees children so beautiful and lively that any one of them could deserve the star;

however, only one will find it. The clear knowledge of faery is reserved for the artist whose talent and perception are, therefore, the gift represented by the star. If we ask the source of the star, the answer is one that leaves room for no further questions: It is ". . . from Faery: that you knew without asking." So the artist's gift is a gift from god, the source of all creation. When Smith and Alf conspire to pass the star on to Nokes' grandson, Tim, they recognize and acknowledge the promise of creativity and imagination in yet another ordinary and unappreciated little boy.

At the same time as the star is a gift from god, it is a gift from other artists. Smith's grandfather had hoped the star would go to him, and he hopes it will go to Tim, of whom he thinks, "So you are my heir." As the father's craft and skill is passed on to the son, the artist's vision and creation go to those who follow him, not simply to copy or imitate (Smith does not know where the star will lead Tim) but as a part of a cultural and artistic heritage that will inform the use to which the gift is to be put.

Envoi

From his early days in the Midlands countryside around Sarehole to his last days as resident honorary fellow at Merton College, Tolkien celebrated with his whole being the importance of the past—to himself, to England, to mankind. In the most personal sense, he mourned for the lost England that had been destroyed by the coming of motorways and housing estates. As early as 1945 in a letter to his publishers about a possible second *Farmer Giles of Ham* he lamented, "The sequel is plotted but unwritten, and likely to remain so. The heart has gone out of the Little Kingdom, and the woods and plains are aerodromes and bomb-practice targets."[1] His ties with the past of England, the very source of his creative vision, depended at least in part on physical surroundings, and he mourned, with the fine irony of the articulate, the shattering of Oxford's repose by the opening of an automobile factory.[2]

As an Englishman, albeit one of unusual linguistic and literary talent, Tolkien felt keenly the lack of a pre-Christian mythology that would reflect the ancient British character. Born of his linguistic studies, this desire for a link to his cultural past resulted in his writings about Middle-earth. He said of his intention, "I had a mind to make a body of more or less connected legend, ranging from the large and cosmogonic to the level of romantic fairy-story . . . which I could dedicate simply: to England; to my country. It should possess the tone and quality that I desired, somewhat cool and clear, be redolent of our 'air' (the clime and soil of the North West, meaning Britain and the hither parts of Europe . . .), and, . . . possessing . . . the rare elusive beauty that some call Celtic."[3]

Finally, Tolkien felt strongly the importance of the human past in defining and permitting that most human and yet most divine activity, artistic creation. Every story, every poem, every language and etymology was for him demonstration of humanity's origins in a greater creator. "Fantasy remains a human right," he wrote in "On Fairy-stories," "we make in our measure and in our derivative mode, because we are made: and not only made, but made in the image and likeness of a Maker."[4]

Notes

1. THE QUEST AS LIFE

1. J. R. R. Tolkien, "English and Welsh," in *Angles and Britons:O'Donnell Lectures* (Cardiff: University of Wales Press, 1963), pp. 36–37.
2. J. R. R. Tolkien, "On Fairy-Stories," in *Tree and Leaf* (London: George Allen and Unwin, 1964), p. 41.
3. Tolkien, "English and Welsh," p. 37.
4. Humphrey Carpenter, *Tolkien: A Biography* (London: George Allen and Unwin, 1977; rpt. New York: Ballantine Books, 1978), p. 34.
5. Ibid., p. 43.
6. Ibid., p. 49.
7. Ibid., p. 55.
8. Ibid., pp. 65–66.
9. Ibid., p. 40.
10. *The Oxford English Dictionary,* compact ed., I, v.
11. S. T. R. O. d'Ardenne, "The Man and the Scholar," in *J. R. R. Tolkien, Scholar and Storyteller,* eds., Mary Salu and Robert T. Farrell (Ithaca and London: Cornell University Press, 1979), pp. 33–34.
12. C. S. Lewis, *The Four Loves* (London: Geoffrey Bles, 1960), p. 78.
13. C. S. Lewis, *The Letters of C. S. Lewis,* ed. W.H. Lewis (New York: Harcourt, Brace and World, 1966), p. 287.
14. Carpenter, *Tolkien,* p. 165.
15. Ibid., p. 180.
16. Ibid., p. 208.
17. Ibid., p. 254.

18. J. R. R. Tolkien, "Author's Preface," in *The Fellowship of the Ring* (rev. ed., New York: Ballantine Books, 1965), p. 14.
19. Carpenter, *Tolkien: A Biography*, p. 282.
20. "J. R. R. Tolkien," in *J. R. R. Tolkien, Scholar and Storyteller,* eds., Mary Salu and Robert T. Farrell (Ithaca and London: Cornell University Press, 1979), p. 13.
21. d'Ardenne, p. 35.

2. THE QUEST AS FAIRY TALE: *The Hobbit*

1. This point of view is suggested in divers sources, including Mary R. Lucas, rev. of *The Hobbit, Library Journal* 63 (1938): 385 and Lillian Hollowell, ed., *A Book of Children's Literature* (New York: Holt, Rinehart and Winston, 1966), p. 184.
2. Philip Norman, "The Prevalence of Hobbits," *New York Times Magazine,* January 15, 1967, p. 100.
3. See, for example, Dorothy Matthews, "The Psychological Journey of Bilbo Baggins," in *A Tolkien Compass,* ed. Jared C. Lobdell (LaSalle, Ill.: Open Court Press, 1975), pp. 29–42.
4. J. R. R. Tolkien, "Valedictory Address to the University of Oxford, 5 June 1959," in *J. R. R. Tolkien, Scholar and Storyteller,* eds. Mary Salu and Robert T. Farrell (Ithaca and London: Cornell University Press, 1979), p. 28.

3. THE QUEST AS LEGEND: *The Lord of the Rings*

1. Randel Helms, *Tolkien's World* (Boston: Houghton Mifflin Co., 1974), p. 21.
2. Joseph Campbell, *The Hero with the Thousand Faces* (New York: Pantheon Books, 1949), passim.
3. Quoted in D. N. Thomas, "Poetry in Translation," *Times Literary Supplement,* January 18, 1980, p. 66.
4. Northrop Frye, *The Secular Scripture* (Cambridge, Mass.: Harvard University Press, 1976), p. 53.

5. Bruno Bettelheim, *The Uses of Fairy Tales* (New York: Alfred A. Knopf, 1976), p. 26.

6. Noreen Hayes and Robert Renshaw, "Of Hobbits: *The Lord of the Rings,*" *Critique* 9 (1967): 58.

7. W. H. Auden, "The Quest Hero," in *Tolkien and the Critics,* eds. Neil D. Isaacs and Rose A. Zimbardo (Notre Dame, Ind.: University of Notre Dame Press, 1968), p. 57.

8. See, for example, Roger Sale, *Modern Heroism* (Berkeley: University of California Press, 1973) and C. N. Manlove, *Modern Fantasy; Five Studies* (Cambridge, England: Cambridge University Press, 1975).

9. Jane Chance Nitzche, *Tolkien's Art* (New York: St. Martin's Press, 1979), p. 123.

10. T. A. Shippey, "Creation from Philology in *The Lord of the Rings,*" in *J. R. R. Tolkien, Scholar and Storyteller,* eds., Mary Salu and Robert T. Farrell (Ithaca and London: Cornell University Press, 1979), p. 307.

11. Shippey, pp. 306–7.

12. Mary Quella Kelly, "The Poetry of Fantasy: Verse in *The Lord of the Rings,*" in *Tolkien and the Critics,* eds., Neil D. Isaacs and Rose A. Zimbardo (Notre Dame, Ind.: University of Notre Dame Press, 1968), p. 173.

13. John Tinkler, "Old English in Rohan," in *Tolkien and the Critics,* eds., Neil D. Isaacs and Rose A. Zimbardo (Notre Dame, Ind.: University of Notre Dame Press), 1968, p. 165.

14. Tinkler, p. 186.

15. Shippey, p. 304.

16. Robert A. Hall, Jr., "Tolkien's Hobbit Tetralogy as 'Anti-Nibelungen,'" *Western Humanities Review 32* (1978): 354.

4. The Quest as Myth: *The Silmarillion*

1. J. R. R. Tolkien, "Beowulf: The Monsters and the Critics," in *An Anthology of Beowulf Criticism,* ed., Lewis E. Nicholson (South Bend, Ind.: University of Notre Dame Press, 1963), p. 70.

2. Erwin Panofsky, *Studies in Iconology* (Oxford: Oxford

University Press, 1939; Harper Torchbooks edition, 1962), p. 58.

3. Jane Chance Nitzsche, *Tolkien's Art* (New York: St. Martin's Press, 1979), p. 129.

4. Quoted in Charles Nicol, "Reinvented Word," *Harper's,* November 1977, p. 99.

5. THE QUEST REALIZED: SECONDARY WORLDS

1. Charles   Nicol,   "Reinvented   Word,"   *Harper's,* November 1977, pp. 96, 99.

2. Quoted in S. T. R. O. d'Ardenne, "The Man and the Scholar," in *J. R. R. Tolkien, Scholar and Storyteller,* eds., Mary Salu and Robert T. Farrell (Ithaca and London: Cornell University Press, 1979), p. 31.

3. Humphrey Carpenter, *Tolkien: A Biography* (London: George Allen and Unwin, 1977; rpt. New York: Ballantine Books, 1978), p. 185.

4. Ibid., p. 185.

5. J. R. R. Tolkien, "Introductory Note," in *Tree and Leaf* (London: George Allen and Unwin, 1964), viii.

6. Carpenter, p. 275.

7. Ibid., p. 276.

ENVOI

1. Humphrey Carpenter, *Tolkien: A Biography* (London: George Allen and Unwin, 1977; rpt. New York, Ballantine Books, 1978), p. 86.

2. J. R. R. Tolkien, *Tree and Leaf* (London: George Allen and Unwin, 1964), pp. 62.

3. Carpenter, pp. 100–101.

4. Tolkien, *Tree and Leaf,* p. 55.

Bibliography

BOOKS BY J. R. R. TOLKIEN

A Middle English Vocabulary. Oxford: Clarendon Press, 1922.

Songs for the Philologists, with E. V. Gordon and others. Privately printed by the Department of English, University College, London, 1936.

Sir Gawain and the Green Knight. Edited by J. R. R. Tolkien and E. V. Gordon. Oxford: Clarendon Press, 1925.

The Hobbit: or There and Back Again. London: George Allen and Unwin Ltd., 1937.

Farmer Giles of Ham. London: George Allen and Unwin Ltd., 1949.

The Fellowship of the Ring: Being the First Part of The Lord of the Rings. London: George Allen and Unwin Ltd., 1954.

The Two Towers: Being the Second Part of The Lord of the Rings. London: George Allen and Unwin Ltd., 1954.

The Return of the King: Being the Third Part of The Lord of the Rings. London: George Allen and Unwin Ltd., 1955.

Ancrene Wisse: The English Text of the Ancrene Riwle. Edited by J. R. R. Tolkien. Vol. 249, Early English Text Society. London: Oxford University Press, 1962.

The Adventures of Tom Bombadil and Other Verses from The Red Book. London: George Allen and Unwin Ltd., 1962.

Tree and Leaf. London: George Allen and Unwin Ltd., 1964.

The Tolkien Reader. New York: Ballantine Books, 1966.

Smith of Wootton Major. London: George Allen and Unwin Ltd., 1967.

The Road Goes Ever On: A Song Cycle, with music by Donald
   Swann. London: George Allen and Unwin Ltd., 1968.
Sir Gawain and the Green Knight, Pearl, and Sir Orfeo.
   Translated by J. R. R. Tolkien. Edited and with a
   preface by Christopher Tolkien. London: George
   Allen and Unwin Ltd., 1975.
The Father Christmas Letters. Edited by Baillie Tolkien. Lon-
   don: George Allen and Unwin Ltd., 1976.
The Silmarillion. Edited by Christopher Tolkien. London:
   George Allen and Unwin Ltd., 1977.

SELECTED SHORTER PIECES

"Some Contributions to Middle-English Lexicography."
   Review of English Studies 1(1925): 210–15.
"Ancrene Wisse and Hali Mei had." *Essays and Studies* 14
   (1929): 104–26.
" 'Sigelwara Land': Part I." *Medium AEvum* 1 (1932):
   183–96.
" 'Sigelwara Land': Part II." *Medium AEvum* 3 (1934):
   95–111.
"Chaucer as Philologist: The Reeve's Tale." In *Transactions
   of the Philological Society* (1934), pp. 1–70. London:
   David Nutt, 1934.
"Beowulf: The Monsters and the Critics." *Proceeding of the
   British Academy* 22 (1936): 245–95.
"Leaf by Niggle." *Dublin Review* 432 (January 1945), pp.
   46–61.
"On Fairy-Stories." In *Essays Presented to Charles Williams,*
   edited by C. S. Lewis, pp. 38–89. London: Oxford
   University Press, 1947.
"The Homecoming of Beorhtnoth Beorhthelm's Son."
   Essays and Studies 38 (1953): 1–18.
"English and Welsh." In *Angles and Britons: O'Donnell Lec-
   tures.* Cardiff: University of Wales Press, 1963, pp.
   1–41.

WORKS CONSULTED

Auden, W. H. "At the End of the Quest, Victory." *New York
   Times Book Review,* 22 January 1956, p. 5.

————. "Good and Evil in *The Lord of the Rings*." *Tolkien Journal* 3 (1967): 5–8. Reprinted in *Critical Quarterly* 10 (1968): 138–42.

————. "The Quest Hero." *Texas Quarterly* 4 (Winter 1961): 81–93.

Beatie, Bruce A. "*The Lord of the Rings:* Myth, Reality, and Relevance." *Western Review* 4 (Winter 1967): 58–59.

Bettelheim, Bruno. *The Uses of Enchantment: The Meaning and Importance of Fairy Tales.* New York: Alfred A. Knopf, 1976.

Blissett, William. "Despots of the Rings." *South Atlantic Quarterly* 58 (Summer 1959): 448–56.

Campbell, Joseph. *The Hero with the Thousand Faces.* New York: Pantheon, 1949.

Carpenter, Humphrey. *Tolkien: A Biography.* London: George Allen and Unwin, 1977. Boston: Houghton Mifflin, 1977. New York: Ballantine Books, 1978.

Frye, Northrop. *Anatomy of Criticism.* Princeton, New Jersey: Princeton University Press, 1957. New York: Atheneum, 1966.

————. *The Secular Scripture: A Study of the Structure of Romance.* Cambridge, Massachusetts: Harvard University Press, 1976.

Grotta-Kurska, Daniel. *J. R. R. Tolkien: Architect of Middle Earth.* Philadelphia: Running Press, 1976.

Hall, Robert A., Jr. "Tolkien's Hobbit Tetralogy as 'Anti-Nibelungen.'" *Western Humanities Review* 32 (1978): 351–60.

Hayes, Noreen and Renshaw, Robert. "Of Hobbits: *The Lord of the Rings*." *Critique* 9 (1967): 58–66.

Helms, Randel. *Tolkien's World.* Boston: Houghton Mifflin, 1974.

Hillegas, Mark R., ed. *Shadows of Imagination: The Fantasies of C. S. Lewis, J. R. R. Tolkien, and Charles Williams.* Carbondale and Edwardsville, Illinois: Southern Illinois University Press, 1979.

Hollowell, Lillian, ed. *A Book of Children's Literature.* New York: Holt, Rinehart and Winston, 1966.

Irwin, W. R. "There and Back Again: The Romances of Williams, Lewis, and Tolkien." *Sewanee Review* 69 (1961): 566–78.

Isaacs, Neil D. and Zimbardo, Rose A., eds. *Tolkien and the Critics.* Notre Dame, Indiana: University of Notre Dame Press, 1968.

Kocher, Paul H. *Master of Middle Earth: The Fiction of J. R. R. Tolkien.* New York: Houghton Mifflin, 1972.

Lewis, C. S. *The Four Loves.* London: Geoffrey Bles, 1960.

————. *The Letters of C. S. Lewis.* Edited by W. H. Lewis. New York: Harcourt, Brace and World, 1966.

Lobdell, Jared C., ed. *A Tolkien Compass.* La Salle, Illinois: Open Court, 1975.

Lucas, Mary R. Review of *The Hobbit. Library Journal* 63 (1938): 385.

Manlove, C. N. *Modern Fantasy: Five Studies.* Cambridge, England: Cambridge University Press, 1975.

Moore, Anne Carroll. "The Three Owls' Notebook." *Horn Book* 14 (1938): 174.

Moorman, Charles. *The Precincts of Felicity: The Augustinian City of the Oxford Christians.* Gainesville, Florida: University of Florida Press, 1966.

Nicholson, Lewis E., ed. *An Anthology of Beowulf Criticism.* South Bend, Indiana: University of Notre Dame Press, 1963.

Nicol, Charles. "Reinvented Word." *Harper's,* November 1977, p. 95.

Nitzsche, Jane Chance. *Tolkien's Art: A "Mythology for England."* New York: St. Martin's Press, 1979.

Norman, Philip. "The Prevalence of Hobbits." *New York Times Magazine,* January 15, 1967, p. 3.

Panofsky, Erwin. *Studies in Iconology: Humanistic Themes in the Art of the Renaissance.* 1939. New York: Harper and Row, Torchbooks, 1962.

Parker, Douglass. "Hwaet We Holbytla . . . ." *Hudson Review* 9 (1956–57): 598–609.

Petty, Anne C. *One Ring to Bind Them All: Tolkien's Mythology.* University, Alabama: University of Alabama Press, 1979.

Purtill, Richard. *Lord of the Elves and Eldils: Fantasy and Philosophy in C. S. Lewis and J. R. R. Tolkien.* Grand Rapids, Michigan: Zondervan, 1974.

Sale, Roger. "England's Parnassus: C. S. Lewis, Charles Williams, and J. R. R. Tolkien." *Hudson Review* 17(1964): 203–25.

————. *Modern Heroism: Essays on D. H. Lawrence, William Empson and J. R. R. Tolkien.* Berkeley, California: University of California Press, 1973.

Salu, Mary and Farrell, Robert T., eds. *J. R. R. Tolkien, Scholar and Storyteller: Essays in Memoriam.* Ithaca and London: Cornell University Press, 1979.

Spacks, Patricia Meyer. "Ethical Pattern in *Lord of the Rings.*" *Critique* 3 (1959): 30–42.

Thomas, D. N. "Poetry in Translation." *Times Literary Supplement* (London), 18 January 1980, p. 66.

Thomson, George H. "*The Lord of the Rings:* The Novel as Traditional Romance." *Wisconsin Studies in Contemporary Literature* 8 (1967): 43–59.

Wilson, Edmund. "Oo, Those Awful Orcs!" *Nation* 182 (1956): 312–13.

Index

MODERN LITERATURE MONOGRAPHS